Talk Box

Talk Box offers teachers tried and tested ways of developing children's talk skills, and provides inspiring lesson plans and fresh, curriculum-based activities which will help children to learn collaboratively through their talk with classmates. At the heart of the activities is the 'Talk Box' – a box of ever-changing interesting objects which provide a focus for class and group discussion.

Talk Box activities are based on these linked ideas:

- Young children need their teachers to help them make sense of the world.
- Talk is children's most effective medium for explaining, discussing and describing.
- Children learn very well from one another when taught how to do so, and are a good resource for one another in the classroom.
- Children may be able to talk but they are not often aware what sort of talk can help them get the best from the education they are offered.
- Straightforward teaching of essential talk skills and understanding should be undertaken in every primary school classroom.
- By becoming articulate speakers, children develop their thinking and reasoning skills.

The activities included in this book are built around specific learning objectives for speaking and listening, and use talk contexts involving subjects such as literacy, numeracy, science, humanities, citizenship and IT. Each activity includes a resources list and suggestions for plenary discussions and extension activities. There are photocopiable worksheets and suggestions for further reading.

Talk Box will help you teach children to engage in the educationally effective kind of discussion known as Exploratory Talk, where everyone's viewpoint is considered, opinions are justified with reasons, and decisions are made together. This revised edition includes new activities, updated curriculum links, current classroom research findings, a home–school link section and a comprehensive introduction to the theory on which Talk for Learning is based.

Lyn Dawes has taught science and literacy for PGCE and BEd courses at Bedford, Northampton and Cambridge Universities, and is a school governor.

Claire Sams has a focus on Special Needs in Education and is currently involved in teaching the Open University course for Teaching Assistants.

Both write from first-hand experience, having taught in primary schools for many years.

Talk Box

Activities for Teaching Oracy with Children aged 4–8

Second Edition

Lyn Dawes and Claire Sams

Routledge
Taylor & Francis Group

LONDON AND NEW YORK

Second edition published 2017
by Routledge
2 Park Square, Milton Park, Abingdon, Oxon OX14 4RN

and by Routledge
711 Third Avenue, New York, NY 10017

Routledge is an imprint of the Taylor & Francis Group, an informa business

First edition published by David Fulton 2004

British Library Cataloguing-in-Publication Data
A catalogue record for this book is available from the British Library

Library of Congress Cataloging-in-Publication Data
Names: Dawes, Lyn, author. | Sams, Claire.
Title: Talk box : activities for teaching oracy with children aged 4-8 / Lyn
    Dawes & Claire Sams.
Description: 2nd edition. | Abingdon, Oxon ; New York, NY :
    Routledge, 2017. | Includes bibliographical references.
Identifiers: LCCN 2016050301 (print) | LCCN 2017012570 (ebook) | ISBN
    9781315627984 (ebk) | ISBN 9781138194137 (hbk : alk. paper) | ISBN
    9781138194182 (pbk : alk. paper)
Subjects: LCSH: Oral communication—Study and teaching (Early
    childhood)—Activity programs. | Communication in education.
Classification: LCC LB1572 (ebook) | LCC LB1572 .D396 2017 (print) |
    DDC 372.62/2—dc23
LC record available at https://lccn.loc.gov/2016050301

ISBN: 978-1-138-19413-7 (hbk)
ISBN: 978-1-138-19418-2 (pbk)
ISBN: 978-1-315-62798-4 (ebk)

Typeset in Palatino
by Swales & Willis Ltd, Exeter, Devon, UK

This book is for Anna, Joshua, Eleanor, Neil and Paul with our love.

Contents

Introduction

The activities in *Talk Box* are based on these linked ideas:

- Young children need their teachers to help them make sense of the world.
- The most effective medium for explaining, discussing, describing and generally making meaning with children is talk.
- Children learn very well from one another when taught how to do so, and are a good resource for one another in the classroom.
- Children may be able to talk, but they are not often aware of what sort of talk can help them to get the best from their education in school.
- Direct teaching of essential talk skills and understanding is straightforward and should be undertaken in school classrooms.

Spoken language in the Key Stage 1 National Curriculum

The National Curriculum 2015 stresses that spoken language skills should be directly taught, saying specifically, 'Pupils should be taught. . .'. Fortunately teachers and the National Curriculum offer rich and varied curriculum contexts for the teaching and learning of **oracy**. By 'oracy' in this book we mean the ability to express ideas clearly and fluently in spoken language. This extract from the National Curriculum 2015 clarifies the range of talk skills that children need to develop:

> Pupils should be taught to speak clearly and convey ideas confidently using Standard English. They should learn to justify ideas with reasons; ask questions to check understanding; develop vocabulary and build knowledge; negotiate; evaluate and build on the ideas of others; and select the appropriate register for effective communication. They should be taught to give well-structured descriptions and explanations and develop their understanding through speculating, hypothesising and exploring ideas. This will enable them to clarify their thinking as well as organise their ideas for writing.

Talk Box provides resources for teaching spoken language skills and strategies for the practice and consolidation of skills, by using talk effectively. The Talk Box book includes:

1. ideas for the direct teaching of talk skills; and

2. activities to help children put their new skills to good use in curriculum contexts.

Talk Box activities are designed to raise children's awareness of the power of productive talk, enabling them to describe, explain and discuss their work together and to develop their individual language and reasoning skills. In essence, *Talk Box* will help you teach children how and why to *think together aloud*.

A Talk Box is a real box (or more accurately, one of a set of boxes) which a teacher uses to hold various resources for different lessons. We suggest you acquire a large plastic box, a big shoe box or a woven basket – anything you think suitable to hold concrete objects which will help start your lessons with a teaching and learning conversation. The activities we suggest in the book can be adapted and developed to suit your class. We suggest that it is possible to use an interactive whiteboard (IWB) as a kind of Talk Box, drawing on the unlimited content of the internet to provide stimulating talk-focused activities. Your children will get to know the Talk Box and what it stands for as they come to know that it contains interesting and surprising things: the resources you use to introduce activities with something new, involving and thought provoking. Whole-class and group discussion will help children to recognise the importance of talk for thinking with others – and to enjoy collaborative learning.

Importantly, theory and research tell us that the chance to think aloud together helps every child to become more adept at thinking individually. The teaching of group discussion skills is therefore a powerful means by which to help a child to develop an individual capacity to reflect and learn. The idea is that from taking part in reasoned discussion, a child can internalise useful ways of thinking which they can employ when working alone. 'Hmmm, what do I know about this? What can I remember? Why do I think this? What might happen, and what should I try? What else do I need to know? Let's think. . .' Such reflection is based on having heard and used similar language with classmates. Effective group work can lead to clearer individual thinking.

The individual child and the teaching of spoken language

The pre-school child learns spoken language from those around them; and very useful this is, providing them with the means to be a member of a community. Once at school, children hear many other ways of talking. But the value of home language is unshakeable – nothing a school offers is better, and nothing can be more important, than what the child already knows about their own talk habitat. What we can provide in school is access to different sorts of talk that may be useful in other settings, ultimately broadening the child's chances to engage with wider society. So, a child will assimilate different accents, dialects and even languages, all by themselves, and know exactly where these fit in their world. They will learn new vocabulary from direct teaching, and hear different ways to put things that they will want to try themselves. Standard English is one of the useful ways of talking that they will add to their repertoire. Exploratory Talk, in which children engage critically but constructively with each other's ideas, is a particularly useful way of talking which they really do need, but will only acquire if it is directly taught and practiced. It is amazing how well the individual child can pick up new ways of talking without having to unlearn any that they have already acquired.

A range of personalities in the talk-focused classroom

Every teacher knows how much children vary. The attributes of the extrovert child – confidence, assertiveness, willingness to speak up – can be so helpful in a classroom, and so rewarding for the child, that we value them highly. Extrovert children are affable, lively and demonstrative, and prepared to take responsibility by contributing ideas. They like having others around them and may be 'bored' by their own company. They have the enviable ability to make small talk.

The introvert child reflects on things and may not speak. Introverted children may evaluate their own thinking, and what they are hearing, so carefully that by the time they have decided what they want to say, the conversation has moved on. As they speak less, they need ever more confidence to break that barrier than their more extrovert classmates. In particular, the `shy' child tends not to speak readily and may be distressed by attempts to encourage this. This can hamper social interaction and can affect learning.

In a classroom where talk for learning is taught, every child benefits. Confident children can see how to reflect and to consider other points of view. Quiet children can experience group work in which they are asked questions courteously and they can offer their idea with complete confidence, knowing that their group mates will listen and respect what is said. Quiet or talkative children may be creative, imaginative or thoughtful; until there is chance to hear what they say, such attributes may not be apparent.

Ways we teach, and the importance of teaching talk

In one method of teaching, the teacher's voice accounts for 80 per cent of the talk in a classroom. The teacher asks questions to which they already know the answer, and some of the children respond. Others sit more or less passively. The teacher explains what one child needs to know to the whole class, and tends to talk over silences: children are under voice control. The class works through a set programme or curriculum.

Another type of teaching involves children responding to one another. This talk is organised and orchestrated by the teacher. Pairs, groups or individuals are expected to think and contribute, staying on task and doing a mix of finding things out, using their memories and creating new learning from what they hear, see and experience. The teacher hears what children understand and do not understand, and takes account of what children have said in planning further teaching. Introductory and closing plenaries provide information, feedback and evaluation, and inform next steps.

In yet another style of teaching, children are told facts, and asked to practice using them until they show competence when tested individually. They are not really required to understand. And in other settings, children are encouraged to choose what they want do, playing freely with one another and the resources and having social (or sometimes unsociable) conversations with no formal learning outcomes expected.

All of these teaching styles or methods can be useful. The real skill lies in deciding which style to use, when and why. Effective teachers have a repertoire of teaching styles and can adapt to the dynamic situation of the classroom in an instant. The least useful option is to simply stick to one style. Perhaps you have attended training courses where the input has been disappointing because the teaching style has seemed inappropriate? For a child, their teacher is with them for an entire school year or maybe even more, and there is no opportunity to fill in a feedback form. Too much woolly 'group work' with classmates who have no idea how to discuss things, or too much sitting in a whole class while the teacher tries to draw out information by use of tedious questioning, or too much free play, can all be dispiriting.

But – children are curious and like to learn. They are also anarchic and disruptive. Teachers have to tap into their curiosity whilst ensuring that children are able to use their most positive creative side in pursuit of learning for themselves and others. One thing that can really give teachers the confidence to make use of a wider range of teaching methods – including those which let the children have a voice – is the knowledge that their class understands the purpose of group work. Teachers who teach children how to use Exploratory Talk have the assurance that a talking group of children are on task, all engaged and learning – rather than hoping that child A is not dominating too much, or knowing that child B won't say a word all day or that child C will subvert the learning opportunity because they want to talk about their new computer game.

Teachers are good at motivating children to acquire new knowledge and develop understanding, and adept at teaching children the skills they need to become creative in their own right. But sometimes the teaching of talk gets left out of the mix, which is unfortunate because it is the one thing that informs all other learning, and is the basis for a child fulfilling their potential – not just in the future, but every day in the primary classroom.

This Talk Box book will help you teach children to engage in the educationally effective kind of discussion known as Exploratory Talk. In Exploratory Talk, everyone's viewpoint is considered, opinions are justified with reasons and decisions are made together. Children listen attentively and feel that they can question or constructively criticise each other's ideas. They invite one another to contribute, asking for explanation, reasons and elaboration. They prolong the discussion until their group can agree on a joint decision.

This sort of talk is very valuable in classrooms because of the way it helps children to reason with one another, clarifying their own thinking and supporting that of their group mates. Reasoning is a robust way of thinking which can support speculation, hypothesis and evaluation. Exploratory Talk helps children to share their own point of view and hear a range of other points of view. Children may not know how to engage in Exploratory Talk since its incidence in social and other settings is rather rare: it only begins to emerge under the right conditions. In class, the 'right conditions' require you, the teacher, and your class to create your own set of **Ground Rules for Talk** for use in discussion sessions. Ground Rules for Talk are a set of rules for talk in group work, generated by a class of children, which support Exploratory Talk. For example, here is a set of KS1 Ground Rules which the class simply called Talk Rules:

Talk rules for our class	We will all join in with the discussion.
	We will invite each other to talk.
	We will listen carefully and think about what we hear.
	We will ask, 'What do you think?' and 'Why do you think that?'
	We will share what we know and don't know.
	We will keep thinking together to come to our decision.

You may be reluctant to impose a set of rules for talk on children. But every child in your class will already have their own, implicit ideas about how they should talk when asked to work with classmates. Such everyday rules may actually put a stop to talk; a child's own internal rules (which may come over as attitudes) might be, for example: 'I only talk, I don't listen'; 'I never speak'; 'I say what I think and take no notice of anyone else's point of view'. When you watch children talking it's easy to discern what rules each is following, everyday ground rules that they have cobbled together from their experience to help them negotiate a rather mystifying world. Their own strategies can help them to cope with many situations, but may not help them to learn. Unless talk rules are openly shared and agreed within your classroom, each child is restricted to their own conception of the nature and purpose of group talk. Widely different assumptions about what it means to talk and work together can generate misunderstanding, disengagement and discord with the result that group work becomes unproductive and frustrating for everyone.

Using a Talk Box approach offers two solutions to these problems:

1. The ground rules that govern talk are made explicit in a way that means they can be worked on, taught and learned.

2. Ground Rules for Talk shared by a class give everyone the chance to make a useful contribution to joint activity and so enable everyone to think and learn together. The rules enable children to take part in the powerful joint experience of Exploratory Talk. As they do so, they can achieve more by working in a group than each child could alone.

Your class Talk Box provides a visual focus and is useful for reminding children that high-quality talk is important in your lessons. We hope that you will be able to provide a suitable box! In practical terms, a cardboard box from the supermarket, or a coloured plastic crate as available in DIY stores, labelled 'Talk Box' and decorated with speech bubbles, talk vocabulary and pictures of people talking, is fine. Chapter 9 in this book suggests a range of other sorts of 'box' for various talk-related purposes.

Grouping your class

Some Year 1 children are best working in pairs initially, because having to respond to two other people can be overly demanding. When children can work in groups of three, mixed-ability and mixed-gender groups provide a sensibly challenging and creative forum for everyone. You know your own class best and will be able to put together groups that are inclusive and in which the children are able to respect one another. Children working in friendship groups tend to agree with one another a little too readily; and you will know which children cannot work together at all, and so need you to teach them the necessary skills. Learning how to get along with everyone becomes more achievable once the talk skills are in place.

What you really require are groups in which there is creative friction without too much ease or too much discord. It is helpful to tell individual children that they have been allocated to groups for very positive reasons so that they understand that both they, and these groups, are special and important. Tell children their positive attributes; for example, that they are good at listening, reading or writing, have good general knowledge, are good at asking questions, good at being encouraging, are sensible, can translate or sign, or know how to include others.

Each group benefits from having a child who can read to a functional level, when possible. Children should be aware that whoever reads, writes, uses the mouse or screen and so on is not their group leader. There is no leader. They should also know that it is inappropriate to compete within their group. The aim of their group is to talk and work together collaboratively so that they all do as well as they can.

Initially, it may be helpful to establish groups, and keep some stability. As the class become more adept at discussion, groups can be altered so that each child has the opportunity to work with every other child in the class. Interestingly, in some classrooms some children may have very little to do with anyone except their friends. Learning to discuss ideas together can address that problem. The class as a unit functions more smoothly when all children see one another as someone they know and someone who will support their learning. Your class Ground Rules for Talk can help to overcome gender and relationship difficulties so that talk with others is always possible, interesting and productive.

Using Ground Rules for Talk regularly

Once established, the class's Ground Rules for Talk should be used for discussion across the curriculum. Exploratory Talk used consistently can become an established part of the class ethos. A clear structure for inclusive discussion has been found to benefit joint writing or art projects, group work at the computer, creative work such as science and design and technology (D&T), learning in mathematics, and in other activities when problem-solving is needed. Interestingly, children who have shared Ground Rules for Talk are also more able to sort out social problems such as playground tiffs.

Chapter 4 of Talk Box provides a structure and suggestions for setting up your class Ground Rules for Talk.

The structure of a Talk Box session

The suggestions for using Talk Box follow this general pattern:

Outline: about the lesson, where it fits in a series of lessons.

Learning intentions to share with the class: (a) curriculum focus, (b) spoken language focus.

In the Talk Box: resources for whole class and group work.

Whole-class input and **group work activities:** including specific discussion points.

Whole-class plenary: re-state the learning intentions and ask the children for feedback on their curriculum work and their talk skills.

Review and extension: what went well, and what needs to be done next.

Extension work: putting what has been learned to use.

Outcomes of Talk Box activities

- Children work more independently, cohesively and collaboratively in groups.
- Children become more aware of how they can use spoken language to think together and get things done.
- Children become better at reasoning and rational decision making.
- Children can raise their group and personal achievement in maths, science, literacy and other curriculum subjects.
- Children develop specific spoken language skills which they can put to good use throughout their education, and in social settings.
- Classes of children know one another better and have more respect for one another's point of view.

Glossary

Ground Rules for Talk A set of rules for talk in group work, generated by a class of children, which support Exploratory Talk.

Exploratory Talk In Exploratory Talk everyone's viewpoint is considered, opinions are justified with reasons and decisions are made together. Children engage critically, but constructively, with each other's ideas. They invite one another to contribute, asking for explanation, reasons and elaboration. They prolong the discussion until their group can account for a joint decision.

Oracy The ability to express thoughts fluently in spoken language.

For more information on talk for learning see the Thinking Together web pages: https://thinkingtogether.educ.cam.ac.uk

Chapter 1   **Talk about talk**

Raising children's awareness of their spoken language as a powerful tool for learning with others.

About this chapter	Children's talk is a distillation and re-purposing of the talk they have experienced. Some children talk fluently from their earliest years; for others talk is difficult. Setting aside specific learning difficulties, some children may not have had the chance to be part of the sort of conversations which will help them speak within a group with confidence, fluency and a good working vocabulary. Talk in school enhances children's spoken language. Talk with peers about a common educational focus is a chance for every child to understand the importance of their own voice, and to learn that communication is an interesting and valuable two-way process. In this chapter, we suggest three specific lessons to raise awareness of talk for learning and to encourage group cohesion, with some extension or follow-up activities.
Activity 1: Talk it up!	Raise awareness of talk as a tool for finding things out.
Learning intention to share with the class	To find out more about a classmate by asking questions and listening.
Whole-class activity	Ask for volunteers to come and choose one of the selection of tools from the Talk Box; hold it up and to say what it is used for. Explain that people make tools to help us do particular jobs well. Show the shoe box and tell children that it is a mystery – we do not know what is inside! Ask children to suggest how we can find out what's inside without damaging it, but using the tools available.

A child will suggest looking into the hole and using the torch because it's black inside. Ask a child to try. Explain that this is a good use of tools: we need the right one for the right job.

Ask one of your confident children (**Leah** in this example) to volunteer for an investigation. Explain that our brains (where we think) are also something of a mystery, like the shoe box – can we tell what's in someone's mind? Why do we need to do so? Can we use any of these tools from the Talk Box? The torch? Stress the danger of light in the eyes. Ask children how we might find out what the volunteer child thinks. Lead children to suggest *asking* him/her, which is the right way to go about it. We can use the tools of spoken language.

Now help the class to investigate what Leah thinks.

Use some starter questions, for example:

> Leah, what's your favourite colour?
>
> Please say yes if you have a bike, no if you haven't.
>
> What are you planning to do after school today?

In the Talk Box

Torch: other tools, for example spanner, screwdriver, garden trowel, paint brush, big ladle, scissors, key, hair brush, scissors – anything unusual you can find.

Shoe box with lid taped down, small hole at one end, small toy taped inside

Model how to listen and respond to the answers.

Ask the class to suggest, ask and listen to further questions and answers, respecting Leah and the way she is prepared to talk about herself.

Explain that by asking Leah to talk, we have found out more about her. She has told us what she thinks about some things. Leah has been good enough to share some information about herself. People might not always want to talk, but in a school classroom, everyone gets on better if there is open sharing. Particular talk tools help us to find out what others are thinking. Questions are useful talk tools, for example the questions, 'What do you think?' 'Why do you think that?'. Knowing about people helps us to understand them. Thank Leah for her help.

Group work

Ask children to talk to one other child. They should take turns to ask each other questions and listen to the answers. They can use the questions already heard, if needed, or provide a definite focus for the talk, such as 'Favourite people', 'Best day ever', 'A story character I like' or 'What I like about weekends'.

Plenary

Ask children to say what they found out about one another. Were there any surprises? Ask for examples of good questions, clear answers and who could be nominated as a careful listener.

Extension

Share some key ideas about spoken language with the children.

1. Explain that we use spoken language – talk – as a tool to find out what's in each other's minds, all the time. Often we do this without really considering what we are doing. We are rarely taught how to talk, but instead pick up our spoken language skills by talking with others. The talk lessons – this is the first one – will help everyone in class to get more out of their talk with one another.

2. We can use reading and writing to find out what people think, but neither is as quick or easy. Writing has benefits. We will go into those another time; for now we will concentrate on talk. Ask children why they think talk is important for learning.

3. Talk is a tool for finding out things about what others and we think; particular language tools are special ways of talking; for example, we can use questions to find things out. We've found out a bit of what's in Leah's mind. Is there more? How can we find out more? By asking questions, listening and encouraging others to talk. What other sorts of talk are there, as well as questions? Other language tools – children might suggest them – are explaining, describing, sharing ideas, giving opinions or reasons, challenging others, agreeing with others.

4. Ask children to consider the relationship of speaking to listening, and talking to thinking. Do we put fully-formed thoughts into words, or do we speak in order to arrange our thoughts?

**Activity 2:
Talking in
my group**

Outline

For the important task of using talk tools together, we need special Talk Groups. Introduce the special talk groups that will help children to work together. The talk lessons are about learning language tools so that we can talk more effectively – for children, you can compare this with learning how to use tools to paint, or how to write using a pencil, pen or keyboard.

You will know your class best. In advance, allocate them to a group with one or two other children; try to mix boys and girls and abilities, and try to avoid friendship groups.

Learning intention to share with the class

To join a group and work together by sharing ideas through talk.

In the Talk Box	Coloured dot stickers
	A selection of small plastic animals/sea creatures/insects/dinosaurs

**Whole-class
activity**

Explain that each child has been chosen for their group because they are good at sharing (give a red sticker); have good general knowledge (blue sticker); are particularly helpful (yellow sticker); or are good listeners (green sticker) (adapt these, or make your own positive criteria). Point out to the children that their groups will have mixed colour stickers because everyone has different abilities and strengths to bring to the group. Call each child to collect a sticker, be congratulated on their strength and to join their group.

Ask children seated with their partner or group to say hello and be ready to listen.

**Group
activity**

Ask a group member to come and choose three animals from the Talk Box without looking. Stress that children cannot swap animals with other groups. Let the children look at these animals with their group and share anything they know about the creatures: names, where they live, what they eat and so on. Now ask the children to think about listening and taking turns. Ask them to take it in turns to tell their group which of the animals they would choose to be their 'group mascot' and why before jointly deciding on an animal mascot. If this isn't possible, leave the choice open for now.

Whole-class plenary: Suggested questions

Can anyone tell us anything interesting they found out about their animals?

Anything you didn't know before?

Anyone give an example of someone who is a good listener?

How well did your group work together?

What should groups do if they didn't reach an agreement?

Were there any problems – what happened – how can the rest of us help?

Can you think of times when it's useful to ask questions?

How did you learn to talk in the first place?

Who doesn't really like talking in groups – can they say why?

Finally ask the class to think about talk. In this lesson, talk has been used to complete the job of choosing mascots. The talk tools in use were questions. During the next lesson the class is going to learn a special sort of talk that will help everyone to do better at school and get on better with people generally. Explain that by working well together we can do better than we could if we worked separately.

Extension activity

Ask groups to write their names or draw pictures of themselves/each other with coloured stickers and a picture of their group mascot.

Find out about other animals that use tools (there aren't many), e.g. chimpanzees, sea otters.

Activity 3: Using questions

Outline

Some children ask questions incessantly. Others may be less familiar with using this way of prompting others to talk. Children in classrooms may get used to being asked questions, and may stop asking questions themselves. In this lesson there is a focus on how and why to ask questions, with the corresponding focus on answering questions. An answer may be that you don't know; it's useful for us to think about what is not known.

Learning intention to share with the class

We are going to think about asking and answering questions.

Whole-class input

Model the group activity by carrying it out with the whole class. Ask the teaching assistant (TA) or helper to select an item from the Talk Box. Now make up questions about the object by talking about:

- What do we know about it?
- What don't we know about it?

| **In the Talk Box** | Select some items (one for each group) from your school's science equipment, for example: magnet, newton meter, torch, magnifying glass, safety goggles, funnel, trowel, sand timer, night light, beaker, measuring cylinder, bug viewer |

You may want to offer some question starters:

How? Why? What? What if?

Tell children that you are going to ask them to make up some questions together, and to remember them till their group is asked to contribute.

| **Group work** | Give each group an object. Allow time for the children to look at it and talk about it, then ask them to focus on their two sorts of questions (finding out what we already know, and what we don't know) and decide what they are going to ask the class. |

| **Whole-class plenary** | Ask each group in turn for a question. You can check if it's a 'We know' or 'We don't know' question. Let the group choose who they will ask for an answer. Encourage any discussion of ideas. Also let the children know that if the whole class reaches a collective 'We don't know' about an object, this is a very useful starter for learning. Ask children for their ideas about how to find out things they don't know. Keep some 'puzzles' open to encourage curiosity. |

Re-state the learning intention. Check what the children think is 'a good question' and why. Ask children how their talk with one another went, and what can be done to help those finding it difficult. Ask children to nominate a good listener, or someone who tried hard to ask questions.

| **Review and extension** | Make a display of the simple 'question words' used in this session, as speech bubbles using children's drawings of themselves or animal pictures. |

Describe and model the use of more complex and targeted question starters:

- how many, how far, how much, how often, how difficult;
- what if, what time;
- when did, which day, why do, who said;
- where was, where will, where should;
- if I;
- would you, will you.

Think of things to put in the Talk Box, e.g. clock, watch, calendar for time-related questions, and use these concrete resources to help groups ask interesting questions. Focus on types of questions and the sorts of answers they elicit. Ask children to reflect on questions they ask that they can answer, and those they ask that they can't.

Ask children to think about how their questions can be answered. Look at questions that can be answered by other children, by looking round the school, by research – in particular books or on the Internet, by asking at home, by imagination. Talk about what questions are appropriate in different circumstances.

Think with the children about answers. Collect answers to a particular question. For example, 'What if the playing field was used to grow vegetables and flowers?'

Sort the groups' answers into those that are imaginative or speculative and those that are factual, or realistic. Talk about the difference.

Compile a list of probing, open questions. Ask children to draw or cut out a cartoon 'talking head' and a speech bubble with one of the questions, e.g. How did you do that? What do you know? Shall we share? Can I help? Where are you going? What do you like? What do you think? Can you tell me more?

Find questions in current reading books and use them to make more speech bubbles for display.

Ask children who have English as an additional language to teach everyone a question in their language, for example: Can I help? How are you? What is your name? What is the time? How old are you?

Talk about talk

Initiate a conversation with talk as the subject.

> Who thinks they are good at talking – can they say why?

> Can you think of times when you are asked not to talk – why is this? Do you agree with it? What is difficult about keeping quiet?

> Can you talk and listen at the same time?

> Do you always think in words? In what other ways can you think? (Consider emotions, pictures, music, numbers.)

Next steps After completing these three introductory activities, the children will have begun to become aware that talk is a useful way to learn and will have practiced some ways to talk together in groups. The next chapter will focus on helping them to understand the importance of listening in this process.

Chapter 2 Listening and thinking

A focus on active listening, to promote the idea of a strong link between listening and thinking. Ways to listen, to become aware of listening and ways to make use of what has been heard.

Outline

In this chapter children consider listening skills and reflect on their own capacity to listen. The National Curriculum requirement is that 'Pupils should be taught to listen and respond appropriately to adults and their peers'. The direct tuition of 'listening' throughout the Primary years helps children to make sense of classroom activities and learning conversations.

Activity 1: Listening and responding

Children consider the importance of listening to a range of sounds.

Whole class

Use the 'mobile phones': ask children to listen carefully while you and your TA/other adult/a child improvise a phone call. Ask children to imagine that you are ringing the zoo trying to find out details about opening times, costs, a picnic room, and types of animals, for a school trip. Ask your helper to simply act 'not listening'; they can hum to themselves, sing, put the phone down, use it to play a game, etc., while you try to get answers to your questions for a minute.

Group work

Ask children to talk to their partner or group about these two ideas, sharing what they think:

> **You can tell if someone is not listening.**
>
> **Listening to some people really is difficult.**

Share group ideas with the class. Ask children to say when they find listening difficult, and when it's easy. Ask why listening is important in the example and then generally, and why listening is especially important for learning.

Repeat the conversation as an example of good listening. Include some questions used in earlier Talk Box sessions. Ask children in pairs to act out the zoo times conversation, or a related conversation; for example, finding out what the café sells for lunch, if the baby tigers are ready to be seen and so on. Choose children to model good listening for the class.

Show the picture of the child crying. Ask children to talk to one another to decide why the child is crying. They can take it in turns to ask questions and offer one another ideas.

Now with the whole class, ask a child to tell everyone what they have **heard**; ask several children this, pointing out how carefully they must have listened.

Ask children who they would nominate as 'a good listener' and why.

In the Talk Box	Two mobile phone handsets (play phones or 'real' but inactive)
	A picture of a child crying

One per group: a small paper bag containing a 'mystery object' (Lego person, plastic animal, packet of seeds, candle, bike clips, sunhat, pound coin, postcard, kitchen item, toy, etc.)

Group work: Talk Box activity

Model or demonstrate this activity then carry it out with the whole class.

Give out the bags and ask one member of the group to look in their bag at the 'mystery object' without revealing it. Their job is to provide clues, and answer questions 'yes' or 'no' as their partner(s) try to guess what the object is. Have a few spare bags so that children can return their bag and collect another one when needed, so that every child has a chance to guess, and to be the 'listener' with the answer.

Ask children to say if they found it easy or difficult to listen to the clues and questions. What makes it easy to listen; what makes it difficult? What can we do to make sure we listen carefully? Why would we need to do that?

Ask a group to repeat their question and answer session (or go through a new set of clues) and show how their work is a model for good listening.

Review

At a later date, check that children can recall what they heard or discussed in this listening session. Use the class collective memory to keep detail fresh and alive in the class consciousness; ask children to think about the link between listening, speaking, thinking and remembering.

Extension

Refer to children's ideas about listening in subsequent curriculum lessons.

Call attention to instances of good listening.

Ask children to take oral messages, to relay instructions to their group, to say what they heard in Assembly or after watching a DVD or other input, or to explain what another child has told them.

Read a story or description and ask children to draw a picture with their talk group, discussing what they heard to add detail.

Ask children to nominate classmates who are good listeners, and say why.

**Activity 2:
Talk for
learning**

Children look at 'ears' and think about the links between hearing, listening, speaking, thinking and learning.

In the Talk Box	Representation or pictures of creatures with large ears, e.g. elephant, cat, fennec fox, rabbit, hare, wolf, donkey, etc.

**Whole-class
input**

Ask children to share ideas about ears, hearing, listening, thinking and learning.

Ask them to come up with a caption for one of the animal pictures which contains at least two of these words.

Ask children to sit very quietly and concentrate on what they can hear. Time 30 seconds and then ask what sounds were heard.

Group work

Ask the group to draw an animal with large ears, then annotate it to show what sounds it might hear. Model an example: draw a donkey (perhaps on a beach) and things around it that may make sound – the sea, children, an ice cream van, a roundabout, a Punch and Judy show, traffic, an aeroplane. Other examples could include a dog on a lead in the park or a fox in a field. Ask children to add noises that the animal should attend to for its own safety, e.g. a dog barking, a pelican crossing, car sounds.

Now ask children to draw a sound picture; that is, themselves as a group in the classroom, and to annotate their picture with sounds they might hear as the school day goes on. Ask them to think about the talk they hear and what learning happens through talk.

Whole class

Ask groups to have a look at one another's sound pictures. Now highlight or colour green all sounds that involve spoken language (talk, singing, TV, computer and so on). Think about the importance of spoken language (talk); ask the children what uses we can make of talk. Bring out the idea of talk for explaining, informing, asking questions, giving answers, instructing, sharing ideas, etc. Use the phrase '**talk for learning**' and ask the children to give examples of when they have learned something by listening.

Extension

Provide scarves or ear muffs. Ask children to wear them for five minutes then report back about the effects of this. An inability to hear can be disorientating and disengaging.

Ask a hearing expert to come in and test children's hearing, or a science sound expert to bring in a machine to test children's frequency range.

Investigate sound volume, using music, to find out what is the lower and upper limit for comfortable listening in class. Measure sound throughout the day to check for variation in volume, and talk about children's suggestions to make sure that the classroom is always a 'listening' environment.

Think about sounds we like and sounds we don't like, and why.

Think about warning sounds, such as a bike bell, pelican crossing, smoke alarm, dog barking, and why they are important.

Activity 3: Listen and repeat

Children think about some listening skills, and role play the effects of each on their learning and that of their classmates.

In the Talk Box	Chime bars and tappers
	Cards numbered 1–10
	Children in three groups – songbirds, rabbits, foxes

Whole class

It's the job of the songbirds to play, the rabbits to listen and the foxes to watch the rabbits. Ask four or five children, the 'songbirds', to sit in a circle with the chime bars on the floor in front of them. Ask one of these children to take a number card from the Talk Box – without revealing the number – and to play a sound pattern with that number of notes. Ask the rest of the class to listen carefully. Now ask a 'rabbit' to say how many notes were played. Ask a 'fox' to say if they agree. Repeat this activity – you can use cards numbered up to twenty if your class is very good at listening, have two songbirds play in sequence, or ask the songbirds to play their number in a rhythm and ask the rabbits to clap the pattern they heard.

Ask the foxes to say who they thought was listening carefully to the music, and how they could tell. Bring out important points about looking, concentrating, not talking, ignoring distractions and being able to answer questions accurately.

Give the children a chance to take on a different role if they wish to.

If the class is adept at this activity, change the conditions. Repeat with everyone talking, or some music playing, or with the songbirds behind a screen or at a distance, or while solving a puzzle. What things are barriers to listening, and what helps people to listen?

Ask the class to come up with a list of five things that make 'a good listener', e.g. a good listener looks carefully, sits still, is not distracted, can say what they heard – and so on. Make the link between listening, thinking and learning.

Group work

Ask groups to talk together to make up two classroom scenes in which one child is teacher and the others are pupils.

Scene 1: the pupils are listening to a story or number lesson.

Scene 2: the pupils are not listening to the lesson.

Film the scenes and watch them together, taking this opportunity to link listening, thinking and learning.

Review

With the whole class, ask the children to talk about the importance of listening, when and why it is difficult, how to concentrate and the impact on learning.

Extension

Start by clapping then move on to using percussion instruments. Ask groups each to devise a rhythm; other groups listen then copy what they've heard using their own instruments. Create a whole-class sound pattern in which the class plays each rhythm in turn. Start by asking a group to play their own rhythm, which the class copies, then pass on to the next group, which does the same. Build up to playing the sound pattern with no interruption. Film this or play for an audience, highlighting the way that the class have listened to one another carefully.

Make a 'sound map' of the school and school grounds.

Create a display based on key words '**think**', '**listen**', '**talk**', '**learn**' using animal pictures and children's drawings of themselves. Refer to this when a focus on listening is needed.

Activity 4: Listen and explain

Tie listening skills in to your topic work. In our example the topic is 'Light and shade' and the focus is on sharing new vocabulary and putting it to use.

In the Talk Box

One per group: torch, 2D shapes, lolly sticks, masking tape

Set up a screen or arrange a blank area of wall for children to make shadows.

Ask groups to make shadows using their Talk Box equipment. They can tape shapes together, and use the lolly sticks to create a 'puppet' effect if they like. They can make up a story or just make shape shadows. Share ideas with the whole class.

Now introduce some relevant science vocabulary: 'light', 'dark', 'shadow', 'bright', 'clear', 'light source', 'transparent', 'opaque', 'reflect'.

Provide these words on word cards. Ask the groups to make up a science demonstration, using their equipment, to show other groups what the science words mean. Use the words in sentences to describe what they can make happen.

Review

Talk together to draw and label a picture of shadows on a sunny day using key words. Ask children to say how talking and listening helped them to learn.

Extension

- Show and talk about the difference between having an object nearer to the light source or further away.
- Using a shop catalogue, ask children to cut out lots of pictures of light sources – TV, computer, lamps and lights, an open fridge, some kettles, LED equipment, etc.
- Talk about the sun as a source of light and the moon as a reflector.

Sort out key words for your topic and help children to hear them in use in a range of contexts, and to use the words themselves as they talk to one another. Use the vocabulary in written work.

Activity 5: Listen and tell a story

In the Talk Box/ whole class	Either use the interactive whiteboard (IWB) or your Talk Box. The children are going to listen to a story lasting no more than five minutes.
	Find a story which is read aloud, online. Choose a story which is read simply and clearly, and is relevant and interesting for your class, or find a story book.

Explain that the class is going to hear the story straight through without stopping so that everyone can listen carefully. You might want to provide the names of the key characters in advance if the children are not familiar with them. Tell the children that they can ask questions at the end of the story.

Read or show the story.

Whole class

Ask the children if they want to ask a question. Encourage others to answer any questions raised. Explain that the story is now in everyone's mind, but that it would be good to share with parents or another class. Ask the class to think about the story – they are going to share what they heard.

Take a few minutes to model this sharing; children should be taught to use positive language, take turns, encourage one another and generally to treat one another's oral contributions with respect. Situations where children dismiss one another's ideas or point out only what is wrong are best avoided. You could devise a short role play with your TA showing effective group talk, and ineffective group talk. Use of the comments 'No!' and 'You're wrong!' for example, can be banned in a humorous way, but with serious intent.

Group work   Read the first line of the story again. Ask children to tell each other how the story goes on from this point: the start of the story, then the middle, then the end. Encourage the children to add detail or particular words they heard, and to help each other to remember the order of things; who said or did what; what they saw in the pictures or on screen and 'what happened next'. There is no need to write or draw anything at this point.

Whole class   Start with a confident child: ask them to start off the story. Ask for volunteers to say what happened next. Build up the whole story, backtracking and adding detail where individuals or groups recall something. Comment on good memory, good listening and supportive group contributions.

Review   Read or play the story again. Afterwards, ask children to say if the class version missed anything important out. Can they evaluate how well they listened?

Ask children to say how their group worked to recover memory, to remind one another and to help share their memory of the story with the class.

Extension
- Ask groups to each draw one scene of the story for display.
- Repeat this listening activity with a non-fiction text and ask children for their opinions: was it easier or more difficult?
- Ask children to tell the story to someone at home, and bring you a one-sentence written comment from their listener.
- After a week, ask the children to repeat the activity of group recall. Is it easy?
- Repeat the activity with a story written by a member of the class, or a poem.
- Ask children to tell you a story they have heard out of the classroom.

Next steps   After completing the activities in this chapter the children will have developed their understanding of what makes a good listener, why it is important to listen carefully and how this is an important part of talk for learning. They will have developed their listening skills. In the next chapter we focus on how children can talk together in groups.

Chapter 3 Me and my group

Establishing coherent groups in which children know how to ask one another questions, listen to one another and think together. The difference between friendship groups and talk groups. Working through problems that arise with group activities.

Shared ideas in our class

In the Talk Box	In three separate bags: 1. a packet of biscuits, an apple, a packet of crisps. Name label or lolly stick for each child; 2. items of sports equipment that represent three or more sports, e.g. football, swimming, gymnastics; 3. boxes of three or more computer games or DVDs. Three large hoops.

Learning intentions

To use talk to identify preferences and find out whether these are shared.

To categorise on the basis of reasons.

To build group understanding.

Whole-class work

Arrange the three hoops on the floor so that they intersect. Alternatively, use circles on the IWB. Label with the names of the foods ('Apples', 'Biscuits', 'Crisps'). Ask a child to hold up and name the foods from the Talk Box. Ask the class each to talk with a partner to decide which of the three foods they like best or if they like two, or all three, equally. Ask one child at a time to choose where to place their name within the hoops – there are seven positions to choose from (A, B, C, AB, AC, BC, ABC). Ask children to put their name card or lolly stick in the area they choose. Talk with the children about preferences, shared likes and dislikes, and shared ideas generally. Use positive language to indicate that opinions are interestingly personal and that hearing the ideas of others helps us to understand them better. Some children may be able to give reasons for their ideas, using 'because. . .'

Next, use labels relating to the sports you have chosen (e.g. football, swimming, gymnastics) and repeat the hoops and choices activity. Finally, repeat the activity using a set of computer games or DVDs that your class are familiar with. Ask the children to talk about preferences and opinions using reasons. See if anyone can identify an idea that they hadn't thought of before, or an interesting reason that might even make them consider changing their mind. Ask children to decide where to put their name label if they do not like any of the choices. Ask children to join a group with shared preferences to put together a one-minute presentation, 'I like. . . because. . .', in which every child speaks as they present to the class.

Group work

Explain that the groups are going to use talk to share some information by talking together. They are going to think aloud about their hobbies, interests, pets and out-of-school life. Display the following question:

What do you like doing when you are not at school?

Model this activity by talking to your TA or a child. Take it in turns to ask one another the starter question. Remind children to ask for reasons: 'Why do you like that?' and for further explanation or details. Children should try to find something that they both like to do; if this is 'watching TV', ask children to be much more specific about programmes and characters.

Ask the group to identify one or two hobbies or interests that they have in common with each other and be able to talk about them.

Whole-class work 2

Ask children to share their 'interesting hobbies' and those of their group with the rest of the class.

Ask the class to evaluate the quality of their group talk: how well did you talk together? Who asked a question? Can anyone remember a reason someone gave? How did you remember to take turns, and to listen carefully? How has concentrating on speaking and listening helped everyone with this activity?

More group cohesion activities

Learning objective

To reinforce questioning, sharing ideas and reasons, and respecting the opinions of others.

Ask each child to draw round their hands on a piece of A4 paper – or, do this with one child in advance and photocopy the sheet. Each child should have a clear outline of a pair of hands.

1. Picture hands

Ask children to write their name at the top of their sheet. They are going to collect 'logos' or small illustrations drawn by all the other members of the class in the hands.

Each child now thinks of one small thing that they like and feel confidently able to draw (e.g. a football, worm, cat, pattern, dog, house, flower, alien, t-shirt) and creates a small pencil line drawing of this next to their name. This can be an object of the child's choice or can follow a theme you might provide such as animals, sports, toys, characters. This should be no bigger than 2 cm square. Once they have added a drawing, children invite others to draw on their sheet and are themselves invited. Drawings should be done carefully, and initialled or signed.

Allow time for collecting contributions and then ask children to say what they like about the picture they have ended up with.

The children should be aware that they are discussing what is being offered, taking decisions and valuing one another's contributions. The picture hands themselves are not the main outcome, although they can be coloured and displayed if there is free time.

2. Sorting things out

Learning objective

To give the reasons used to group things.

Resources

Lay the three labelled hoops on the floor so that they intersect – or use IWB graphics.

Ask a child to take an item out of the Talk Box and put it where they think it goes in the hoops. As they place the object, they should give a reason why.

Ask for alternative suggestions about where that object could be placed. For example, does a pencil fit best in the reading, writing or number hoop? Or is it better placed where writing and number overlap? Why? Which objects could go in more than one place?

In the Talk Box

A collection of about ten classroom objects, e.g. scissors, ruler, Multilink, book, CD-ROM, pencil, felt-tip pen, dictionary, rubber, sharpener, stapler

Three large hoops with labels: 'Reading', 'Writing', 'Number'

Other blank labels

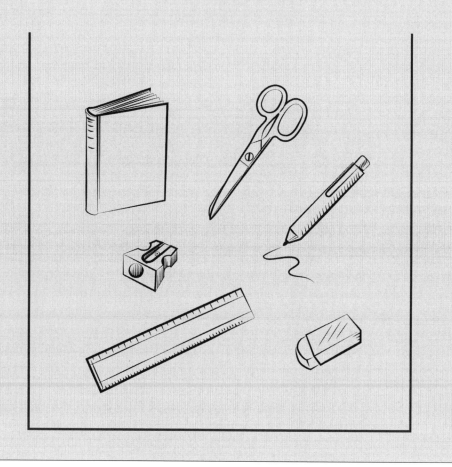

Repeat with new labels. For example you could use the labels 'Plastic', 'Metal', 'Wood' or 'Bendy', 'Shiny', 'Hard'. Show that if we change the group (category), we change the way things are sorted.

Other contexts

This talk-based activity can be used across the curriculum. Some examples:

Science: sorting and classifying materials, or living things.

Literacy: considering attributes of story characters, e.g. whether the characters are kind, unlucky, friendly, bad, good, happy, etc.

Maths: sorting numbers, e.g. in the 2× table; odd and even; 2D shapes.

Next steps

The children have had experience of working together in special groups that use talk to solve problems. They are ready to create and agree their Ground Rules for Talk which will ensure that group work generates Exploratory Talk to get things done together. This will be the focus of the next chapter.

Chapter 4 Your class Ground Rules for Talk

Creating a set of Ground Rules for Talk with the whole class, which, when in use, will ensure that group work generates Exploratory Talk. Taking pride in spoken language and putting talk to work to get things done together.

Children learn to talk in school. They learn vocabulary, ways of expressing ideas, new uses for talk, new phrases and ways to emphasise what they want to say. Children learn and practice talk out of school, but for many children the classroom is the place where they will hear models of talk that will help them to think and learn. Importantly, they need to understand how members of a group can discuss things in an inclusive, rational way. The idea of talk as a tool for learning together must be explicit. Children who feel that they are likely to be ignored, gratuitously corrected, belittled or laughed at because of what they say, will say very little. Or perhaps they will make a joke, or throw in a social comment intended to lead the talk back to easier ground. This is what can make group work ineffective. Children are responsive to those around them and well aware of the risk of sharing ideas with others, but social unease should not hinder learning: once a class has been taught how to make group talk rational, equitable and orderly then everyone is more likely to join in.

The security of shared Ground Rules for Talk allows freedom of expression, equality and openness. The rules make learning possible for groups of children working together with no supervisor or adult present to act as 'referee'. The group with shared rules works in a determined atmosphere of mutual respect and has an expectation that they will hear a range of interesting points of view to consider. The chance to compare and contrast their own ideas with those of others is daunting, but exhilarating. The opportunity to listen, and be listened to, is unusual and engaging.

Every class needs to create its own specific Ground Rules for Talk so that the children relate to them and agree that each rule is a good idea. Children must be helped to suggest rules and compile a working list that will support their talk work in groups.

The term 'ground rules' usually refers to rules that are never made explicit, and which may never be understood or even noticed. For Talk Box activities, we take the ground rules that underpin group talk and make them clear to each child, so that things can go as they should. It is obscured, mismatched and contradictory ground rules in separate minds that confound children when they set out to talk to one another in a serious way. It's not easy to share and negotiate ideas, beliefs, feelings and hypotheses, but once the children have shared Ground Rules for Talk all of this becomes much more possible. Being part of a group that is really discussing interesting things is very inspiring for a child. The Ground Rules make this possible in an everyday way, helping the child to learn while remaining curious, open and articulate about their experience of the world.

Whilst learning to talk, children are also learning to become socialised, educated and thoughtful young people, able to listen to and consider a range of points of view, able to express their own ideas and able to use and evaluate reasons in order to make decisions.

Here's an example of Ground Rules for Talk in a group. Talk based on these rules is likely to be Exploratory Talk.

Ground Rules for Talk	Everyone should be asked to speak
	Everyone should listen carefully
	We will ask for, and give, reasons
	We can agree or disagree
	Everyone respects what is said in the group
	We will share what we know
	We will agree on what the group thinks

The following rules were generated by a Year 2 class after taking part in activities such as those in Chapter 1 of this Talk Box book.

Our Talk Box Ground Rules	1. Co-operate – try to get along with each other.
	2. Take turns to talk and to listen.
	3. Share your thoughts.
	4. Ask for reasons.
	5. Think together about everyone's ideas.
	6. Try to agree what to do together.

You can see that this class has used the idea of the Talk Box in their title, has numbered their list and has included the ideas of 'co-operation' and 'thinking together' as reminders to themselves. These are their own ideas, and the rules are expressed in their own language. The rules meant something special to this class. Although it might seem simpler to provide ground rules and ask the class to apply them, it's so much more effective if a class 'owns' their rules and believes in them.

The following section of this chapter sets out some activities you can use in order to create, establish and practice use of Ground Rules for Talk.

| **Activity 1: Our Ground Rules for Talk** | In this crucial activity, you and the children generate a set of Ground Rules for Talk which they can use in group work. |

| **In the Talk Box** | Sports and/or game equipment, e.g. a bat, ball, swimsuit, baseball cap, board game, toy car, handheld computer, dice |
| | Large pieces of paper and marker pens for each group |

Talk Box discussion

*The aim of this whole-class discussion is to ensure that children are aware that **rules** are very valuable. They are not just restrictions, but can help groups of people to be safe (e.g. in cars) or help things to be fair (e.g. in a team game).*

Briefly explain the aim of the activity. Ask a child to take an item from the Talk Box. As each item is brought out ask the children to suggest a 'rule' that might be associated with the sport/game it represents, and to say what might happen if the rule was scrapped or changed.

- Introduce the concept of 'ground rules' as basic rules that everyone knows and shares, if the sport or game is to work for everyone.
- Discuss the reasons for rules emphasising those to do with safety or fairness.
- Ask children to suggest changing a rule and thinking what would happen, e.g. going down ladders and up snakes; sharing out all the monopoly money; being able to throw a football as well as kicking it; buying cheats for computer games.
- Discuss and consider what would happen if only some of the players agreed to the new rules. Bring out the idea that rules don't work unless everyone agrees to use them.
- Use the swimsuit to talk about rules for behaviour at the pool, and the car to ask the children if there are rules for being a passenger as well as being a driver. Ask children to think about how they learned these rules. Some of them are rarely made explicit but are actually well known (e.g. no eating in the pool, not to touch the hand brake).
- Rules can change, e.g. it used to be a common rule that swimmers must wear caps. Ask the children if they have rules at home, for example: for using the TV remote; using their mobile; for helping themselves to a snack; for bedtime or rules to do with talking, going outdoors, or pocket money.
- Ask children what they think about archaic rules, for example, that until relatively recently some children were not allowed to talk at the table, shops were not allowed to open on Sundays, and children were not allowed in pubs.

Sum up the importance of rules, and the idea that we know some rules without having them written down or even talked about.

Pair or group discussion

Ask children to think about who they like to work with in class: not their best friend, but someone they can rely on to help and support them. Ask children to work in self-choice groups of up to four.

Tell the children that they are going to suggest ways of working that will help everyone to do well in class. You could have four groups, each talking about one of the issues. Ask the groups to talk together to share ideas: What does the group think about these ideas? Do they agree or disagree, and why? Can they prepare to tell the rest of the class what their group thinks?

Talking Points: Talk in class

Listening is difficult and most things you have to listen to are boring.

Sharing ideas wastes time and it is better to get on with things on your own.

If you don't know something, it is best to pretend you do know.

Talk is not work for us in school – only reading, writing and maths are work.

After discussion, help children to share ideas with the whole class. Help them to bring in examples of talk from previous activities. Encourage the children to consider the idea that talk helps thinking. Bring out the ideas that in group talk all opinions will be valued, that questions must be asked and that all opinions must be backed up by a *reason*.

Activity 2: Deciding on our Ground Rules for Talk	Provide or display a copy of p. 90 **'Are these useful Ground Rules for Talk?'** or print on cards. Ask a reader to read out each box in turn, then ask the groups to talk together, giving opinions and reasons, to decide whether they think the rule is: a) a sensible rule for group talk for learning – if so, colour green; b) not a sensible rule – if so, colour red; c) they are unsure or undecided, remembering that it is fine to be undecided – if so, colour orange.

Ask each group to report back on their opinions. You might want to fill in a tally chart so that the children can see which rules everyone agrees are 'green'.

Use this information to decide on a straightforward class set of Ground Rules for Talk: six or so is plenty. Ask the children to say the rules in their own words, or alter first drafts to make them just what they want.

Ask the children if they think it is a good idea to agree to use these class Ground Rules for Talk when working in groups. How would it help? What would be difficult about it? Are there any further suggestions or modifications?

Make a poster, screen or handout of the rules for display in the classroom.

Provide copies for children to take home. Ask parents for their response.

Refer to and rehearse the rules before talk sessions, and use plenary time to ask children who helped them to learn through talk.

Ask children to collect examples of when the rules have been useful to share with you and the class.

Activity 3: Practicing using Ground Rules for Talk

Read the story, using the things from the Talk Box at appropriate points.

Allocate a 'scene' from the story to each group, for example (seven groups):

> Liffey at home
>
> Liffey sets off on the shopping trip
>
> Liffey plays skipping with Bracken the rabbit
>
> Liffey plays football with Dribble the dog
>
> In Uncle Raggy's shop
>
> Liffey arrives home with the shopping
>
> The tea party.

Share Ground Rules for Talk and remind children to try to use them.

Ask each group to talk together to create an illustration of their scene with a caption and one or more speech bubbles, to share with the class.

In groups, the children decide how to create their picture. For example, they can all draw on one large piece of paper; they can draw and cut out separate bits of the scene; they can use the computer; they can paint, draw a cartoon or make a 3D model in plasticine. The group must agree and bring you a plan before they proceed. Set a time limit for planning.

Share the illustrations and ask children to provide examples of good co-operation, discussion, giving reasons, listening and negotiation. If there were problems, ask the class to suggest what could be done differently. Ask groups which of the Ground Rules they think they were best at using. Were there any that they found hard? Do they think that they did better as a group than they could have working alone?

Display the illustrations in the story sequence, with the children's names attached.

Ask the children if they can remember what Liffey decided at the end of the story.

Further writing activities can be based on the illustrations and discussions. For example, you can create a slide show and children can write captions and speech bubbles. Groups might add an extra scene, decide on the backstory of one of the characters or make an animated film using plasticine. Groups can put themselves, or their choice of character, into the story by re-writing it as if they have been asked to collect some equipment from another classroom. For each activity, the contribution of classmates through talk can be emphasised.

In the
Talk Box

Short story: *Liffey's Shopping Trip*

Provide or display a copy of p. 94 **'Liffey finger puppets'** or print on cards

Cat toys or pictures

Purse, backpack, a packet of butter, a pot of strawberry jam, a box of sugar cubes and some peppermint tea

Liffey's shopping trip

Liffey was a grey, stripy kitten. She wore a red collar and a red woolly hat with holes for her ears. One afternoon Mother Cat, who was called Mittens, was getting everything ready at home, because her friends Tibby and Rollo were coming to tea.

'I have to get out my best cups and make a cake,' said Mittens, who was in a great rush, because she had sat out in the sun all morning.

'Oh Liffey, run along to Uncle Raggy's shop for me. Yes! Quickly! I need a little packet of butter, a pot of strawberry jam, a box of sugar cubes and some peppermint tea.' She was washing up cups, and having wet paws always made her cross.

Liffey thought this shopping list sounded a bit much.

'Will you write it down for me?' said Liffey.

'No, no, you silly kitten, I don't have time. Here is the money in a purse. Make sure you don't lose it. You can put it under your hat.'

'I will put it in my backpack actually,' said Liffey, who thought she would look really peculiar with a purse under her hat. So she put on her backpack, which she liked because it matched her collar, and set off through the woods to the shop.

As she skipped along she practiced saying to herself,

'A packet of butter, a pot of jam, a box of sugar cubes and some peppermint tea!'

By the hedge she met her friend Bracken, a small but rather energetic rabbit whose main idea was to keep jumping about.

'Where are you going, Liffey?' asked Bracken. 'I have a new skipping rope. Come and play!'

'I am in a hurry,' said Liffey, importantly. But the skipping rope did look fun. 'Oh well – I suppose five minutes won't matter.' So she put the backpack down on the grass and skipped and hopped with Bracken. It was quite a bit longer than five minutes before she remembered the shopping trip.

'Oh! Yes! I'm in a hurry!' And she collected her backpack. 'Bye, Bracken! Now let me think – it was mint, I know it was, definitely mint, and a packet of butter, a little pot of jam, a box of pepper and some strawberry sugar please!'

Bracken listened to this list and felt very puzzled.

In the field near the shop she met her friend Dribble the puppy who was, as usual, very enthusiastic and keen to dash around.

'Where are you going Liffey?' said Dribble. 'I have a new football. Come and play!'

'I am in a hurry,' said Liffey, importantly. But the idea of playing football did sound fun. 'Oh well – I suppose five more minutes won't matter.' So she put down her backpack and dashed about with Dribble, kicking the football for much longer than five minutes before she thought about the shopping again.

'Whoops!' she said. 'Oh yes, I'm in a hurry! Bye Dribble! Let me see. What am I supposed to get? A cube of pepper, a little buttermint, a box of jam, some sugar mice and some strawberry tea. . .' Dribble looked at her in confusion and she suddenly felt a bit wobbly. The shopping list seemed to be a bit less organised than it had when she set out.

But finally, the shop door, and here she was! Liffey was quite out of breath as she pushed the door open. In the shop it was dark and cool and rather quiet. Liffey remembered why she didn't like the shop very much. She hopped uneasily from paw to paw. The shop was owned by the big ginger cat Uncle Raggy. At the counter Mr Slowly the snail was spending ages choosing just the right shade of varnish for his shell. He was very fussy. Liffey took the purse out of her backpack and fidgeted about.

'Let's think,' she said to herself, a bit flustered. 'It's a good job I've got such a brilliant memory. I know just what I need – pepper and jam, butter and ham – or strawberry tea – oh dear!'

Eventually Mr Slowly paid for his varnish and slid out of the shop door.

'All right, young Liffey. What can I get for you?' said Uncle Raggy.

'Ok,' said Liffey, trying to be brave. 'Right. Here we go. I want some pepper pots, some mint cubes, a box of blocks, some strawberry mice, a packet of buttercup jam and. . . oh what was it. . . some tea? Some something tea please!'

Uncle Raggy looked a little surprised. First he frowned and then he shook his head in a way that made his ears rattle. It certainly was quiet in the shop. Liffey shuffled her paws. Uncle Raggy was so solemn and serious. 'And of course I'm in a hurry,' she told him, just so that he would realise how important it was.

'A hurry. I see. Tea. Well, give me your backpack and I'll put everything in,' he said. 'Oh dear, oh dear. I don't think we have many of those things. . . what did you say? A box of socks. . . some ice cream mice. . .' He nodded as he put things in the bag.

What would Mittens say if she went home with ice cream mice? Liffey was almost sure it didn't sound quite right. She began to mew. She put her paws over her eyes and rubbed her ears, but it didn't help. She was all muddled: was it ice or mice? And where did the cubes come in?

'Oh I know! It must be ice cubes!' she said excitedly. 'And I mustn't lose them! I must carry them under my hat!'

'Ah yes, of course you must,' said Uncle Raggy, carefully packing her purse on top of the things he had put in her backpack. 'Ice cubes under your hat. A good idea. Maybe it will make your ears stiff and help you be a good listener, just like me.'

He wrapped some ice cubes in a plastic bag.

'Here you are; under your hat. I reckon you'd better go straight home!'

Too embarrassed to refuse, Liffey took the ice cube bag and shoved at it till it fitted under her hat. It did not feel good. She managed to whisper 'Thank you' in her smallest voice before he lifted the backpack onto her shoulders – it felt sort of heavy, hard and full of corners. She almost dashed out of the shop. She felt horrible. Her ears were frozen. She must get home. This was a nightmare. In the field Dribble called her and kicked the ball towards her but this time she ignored him. Icy water was running under her collar. By the hedge Bracken waved the skipping rope enticingly, but Liffey shook her head, which made trickles of ice slither down her nose. The backpack was terribly lumpy – it must be the, what was it, potato chips, she thought, or the other thing, the – the red pepper pot – ah, she was home! At last, at last. Liffey bounced into the kitchen and ripped off her red hat.

'There!' she said. 'All the things for tea!'

Tibby, Rollo and Mittens looked at her, astonished by her wet fur and the ice melting everywhere and setting off across the floor.

'But what have you been up to? You were so long we almost gave up,' said Mittens. 'Here, give me the bag.'

'What have you got there, Liffey?' said Tibby.

But Liffey couldn't say. She didn't believe that anyone could have remembered that terrible shopping list. All she could think of was a muddled mixture of how cold her ears were and pepper pots of buttered mice. Mittens opened the backpack, took out the purse, and carefully lifted out all the things that Uncle Raggy had put in.

'Oh! A nice little packet of butter!' she said, sounding very pleased. 'Here we are; a pot of strawberry jam; a good square box of sugar cubes and some lovely peppermint tea!'

The visiting cats nodded and looked satisfied. They began to purr.

'What a good kitten your Liffey is,' they said to Mittens, looking forward to their tea.

Liffey felt the world had been turning the wrong way and had suddenly set off turning the right way again. She went out into the sun to brush her fur. What had happened? What had Uncle Raggy said? She rubbed her ears with her paws. It was something to do with listening? – and he had been right: yes, her ears were nice and stiff now.

More activities to practice children's use of Ground Rules for Talk

Activity 1: Important things to think about

Introduce some key talk tools that will encourage Exploratory Talk. Ask children to use them in their talk, for example:

'What do you think?' 'I think. . . because'

'I agree because. . .'/'I disagree because. . .'

'Could you say a bit more please?'

'Can I. . . can you. . . explain / describe / tell me?'

'I understand. . .' /'I don't understand. . .'

Choose an important topic to think about – a topic of interest to your class, or a current whole-school issue. Ask groups to discuss their ideas using the talk tools. Use plenary time to air ideas about the issue and also to ask for examples of good talk and effective use of the Ground Rules.

Important topics for children to discuss could include:

School uniform and non-uniform days

Helping children in other parts of the world

Keeping the classroom/school clean and tidy

Using areas of the playground at breaks and lunchtimes

Recycling at school and home

Healthy lunch and snacks

What new sports equipment/library books/software to buy

A new art work for the reception area

Inviting adults into school – who could we ask?

Activity 2: Puss in Boots

Find different versions of this traditional story. Ask groups to discuss their opinions of the stories: which they prefer, which has the most likeable characters, which has the best ending and so on. Ask groups to report back and to say how the discussion helped their thinking.

Look at a range of illustrations of Puss in Boots. Compare traditional depictions with contemporary ones; what are the similarities and differences, and what is the artist trying to convey? Which do children prefer and why? Ask groups to draw their own Puss in Boots using ideas (colours, hats, boots, eye size, etc.) that they like best and display it with their reasons.

Use Puss in Boots word cards or a word mat. Ask groups to help one another to read the words, deciding which words are difficult. Ask groups to use the words to make up oral or written sentences, or to tell the story in sequence.

Ask groups to discuss the Talking Points. What does everyone think? Why? Organise a plenary to bring out children's ideas, and to ask for positive feedback on aspects of the group discussion such as listening, suggesting ideas, asking questions or summarising.

Talking Points: Puss in Boots

The miller's son is kind so it's fair that he does well.

This story is bad because it teaches people to tell lies.

Puss' boots are not used at all and so should not be in the story.

Activity 3: Squashing, bending, twisting and stretching

Ask the class to remind one another of their Ground Rules for Talk. The emphasis for this session is on sharing ideas. Ask children how they can organise turn-taking to share everything they know.

<table>
<tr>
<td>In the
Talk Box</td>
<td>For each group, a bag or box containing plasticine, sponge, play dough, clay, elastic bands, Lego, eraser, sponge ball, table tennis ball, paper ball, metal spoons, wooden spoon, cork, plastic toy animal, empty water bottle, squashy toy – a mix of flexible and inflexible materials.</td>
</tr>
</table>

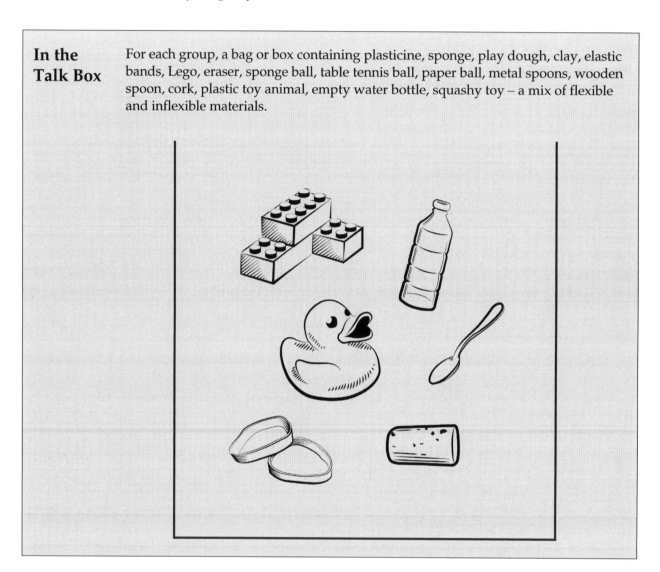

Encourage the children to look at and talk about the materials for a few moments to familiarise themselves with them.

Display, describe and demonstrate the key words '**squash**', '**bend**', '**twist**', '**stretch**' using one of the materials. Explain that:

- these are all forces, versions of a push or a pull;
- some materials change when force is used;
- some change then return to their original shape.

Ask groups to talk together to:

a) group objects depending on 'squashiness' etc.;
b) make up a sentence comparing two objects;
c) complete a chart with object names/the four key words, using ticks to show which can be applied to the object;
d) make a display of objects that they can explain to others using the key words;
e) make a model with the plasticine, using all four key words.

Ensure that children are given the chance to offer positive feedback on their group's use of talk in your plenary session. You can be very specific in requesting examples of effective use of the Ground Rules:

Who asked you a good question?

Did you notice anyone listening carefully?

Can you say who explained something – what did they say?

How did your group reach an agreement?

Who do you think is good at using the Ground Rules?

It's a useful opportunity for children to provide positive feedback for one another, and for individuals to be nominated as 'good at talk' is both reassuring and confidence-building. The steps may be small but the cumulative effect of talking about how the talk went is very powerful.

Next steps

Now that the class Ground Rules for Talk have been established, and children have had a chance to practice using them, this approach to group work can be applied across the curriculum. Exploratory Talk then becomes an integral and important way in which children learn. They can use talk effectively to get things done together. The Ground Rules should be on display and be mentioned frequently. The rest of the book offers suggestions for talk in a range of contexts for you to adapt and use throughout your school day.

Chapter 5 Exploratory Talk in mathematics

Spoken language in the Maths National Curriculum; talking about mathematical concepts and decision making.

Talk Box activities incorporate these three important ideas from the KS1 Maths National Curriculum:

Maths words: The quality and variety of language that pupils hear and speak are key factors in developing their mathematical vocabulary and presenting a mathematical justification, argument or proof.

What we think about maths: Children must be assisted in making their thinking clear, both to themselves and others.

Sharing maths points of view: Teachers should ensure that children build secure foundations by using discussion to probe and remedy their misconceptions.

In addition, children learning mathematics are expected to begin to make connections and move between different ways of representing ideas as they begin to use mathematical language to talk about how to solve problems. They also need to use talk to apply their mathematical knowledge in science and other subjects.

Learning arises from the opportunities the children have to interact with materials, vocabulary and one another's ideas in discussion. The following activities are suggestions and ideas for you to modify for your class. Talk is integrated into the activities.

Number and place value

In the Talk Box	A copy of *The Very Hungry Caterpillar* by Eric Carle.
	(You can find a video of Eric reading this book online.)
	Sets of pictures from the story – one set for each group – showing the days and what was eaten (Monday one apple, Tuesday two pears, etc.)

Maths words

First read the story to recall it together and talk as a whole class about how many things are eaten each day, asking questions such as: 'What would be one more? One less?'

What we think about maths

Provide each group with a picture and ask them to talk together to agree on some mathematical questions about it. Provide key phrases, such as 'how much', 'one more', 'one less', 'altogether'. For example, the children might ask 'How much has he eaten today?' 'What would be one more than this?' Or the children can create statements such as 'One less than this would be two'. Write ideas on speech bubble shapes and arrange around the picture. Carry on to another picture.

Sharing maths points of view

Ask groups to discuss how to organise their pictures into a sequence. Ask questions such as: 'Which is first? Second?' to practice the language of ordinal numbers.

**Number:
Addition and
subtraction**

In the Talk Box	A plastic balance for each group with an equal sign on the fulcrum
	A collection of objects of equals size such as Duplo blocks, Numicon or Multilink

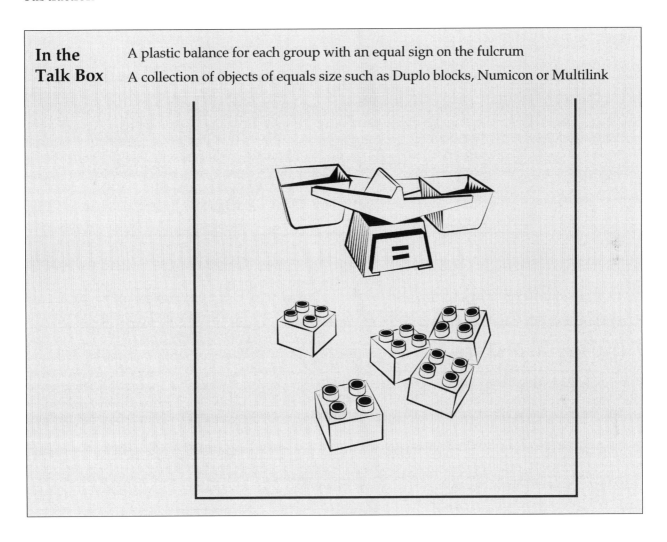

Maths words

Ask one child to put a different number of blocks in each pan of the balance. Talk with the class about balancing: how could we make it balance – by adding or taking away – so that each side is equal?

What we think about maths

In talk groups, use the objects and balances to make up sums and agree how to write these using the mathematical symbols + – = (such as 3 + 2 = 5, 3 = 5 – 2).

Ask groups to write ideas on separate cards.

Sharing maths points of view

Swap cards between groups and ask children to discuss and 'test' the sums. Then the groups can use the cards to create number stories with mathematical language.

Extension

Use the IWB to display simple equations, some of which are correct and some which are not. Ask groups to talk together to sort these into correct and incorrect, using their balances and mathematical language to explain why. They can go on to find ways to put right the incorrect equations, or explain their thinking to other groups, or make up number stories.

Number: Multiplication and division

Teddy Bears' Picnic: using sharing, halving, doubling, 'groups of'.

In the Talk Box	A set of two teddy bears, two paper plates, two cups, toy apples, toy cakes, grapes or similar picnic items that can be divided evenly between the number of bears.

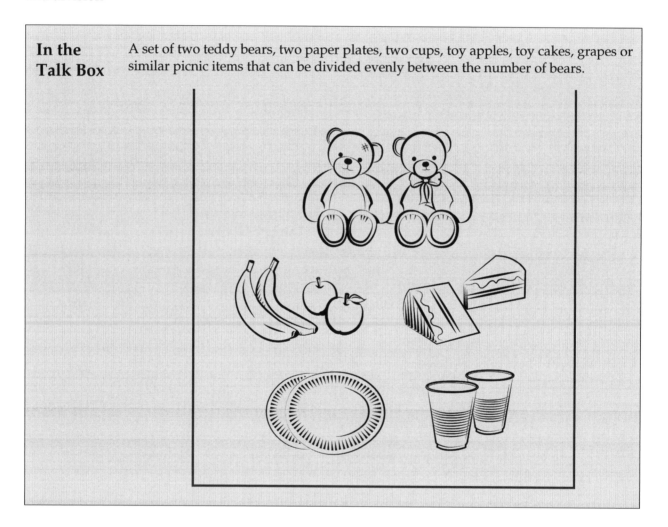

Maths talk

Ask one group to share the picnic equally between the bears.

Set up different groups of bears and food on tables, for groups to talk about how to share out equally. Ask the groups to make sure that each bear has the same amount of picnic food.

What we think about maths

Ask groups to talk together to agree a way to write or draw how they have shared the picnic equally. Children can go on to use bears and food or other combinations of objects to explore the idea of doubling. Model the language use, 'One bear needs . . . two bears need . . .' A digital camera can be used to record doubling, showing how a pattern might be continued.

**Number:
Fractions**

In the Talk Box	A bag for each group containing a selection of half of a picture or half of a shape. The other halves should be mixed through other groups' bags, so that it is possible to assemble complete shapes by talking with other groups.

Maths talk

Ask groups to talk with other groups to describe carefully what they have 'half of'. By talking, find and match equal parts to make a whole. Swap with other groups so that all pictures and shapes are arranged to make whole ones.

What we think about maths

Agree some sentences with the group to describe the pictures/shapes. For example:

It is made of two equal pieces.

It has two halves.

Two halves make one whole.

Sharing maths points of view

Give groups half of a picture/Lego model, etc. and ask them to complete it to make a whole.

These 'jigsaw' activities could also be carried out using quarters, or a mixture of both half and quarter pictures.

**Measurement:
Mr Slowly's
day**

This activity is about sequencing events in chronological order using language such as 'before', 'after', 'next', 'first', 'morning', 'afternoon', 'evening', 'night'. It develops the spoken language of maths through discussions using this mathematical vocabulary. It enables children to use talk to provide a mathematical justification for their ideas. The broader requirements for spoken language that this activity addresses are concerned with:

- using spoken language to develop understanding through speculating, hypothesising, imagining and exploring ideas;
- considering and evaluating different viewpoints, attending to and building on the contributions of others.

Sharing maths points of view

Ask the groups to discuss the Talking Points and agree on a way to put the cards in order. Compare their ideas with other groups' and see if there are different ways to arrange the cards.

Extensions

Similar activities can also be done with life cycles of plants, frogs, etc.

Children can arrange pictures of the playground at different times of day: before and after school, at break and lunchtimes, during lessons, after-school clubs, sports activities, etc. and match these to clock faces showing the time it could be.

In the Talk Box	(This activity uses a character from the Liffey story in Chapter 4.)

A set of cards for each group with statements about Mr Slowly's day:

- It is hot and sunny. Mr Slowly is inside his shell under a nice cool stone.
- It is dark. The moon is shining. Mr Slowly slides his way along the path.
- It is just getting dark. Mr Slowly comes out from under the stone and finds a nice, tasty lettuce leaf.
- It is early morning and there is a shower of rain. Mr Slowly moves along the row of lettuces, nibbling through six green leaves.
- A blackbird wakes up. He is hungry and would like to eat a fat snail for breakfast. Mr Slowly slides behind a plant and waits inside his shell.
- It is afternoon. Mr Slowly is feeling hungry again and peeps out of his shell, but it is still too hot for snails to be moving about.

A set of Talking Points for each group:

Talking Points: Mr Slowly

This is the first part of Mr Slowly's day because . . .

Mr Slowly is asleep in the afternoon.

Mr Slowly has eaten the lettuce leaves, the next thing he does is . . .

Before it gets hot there is a shower of rain.

After it cools down, Mr Slowly wakes up.

Geometry: Properties of shapes – 3D shapes	This is an activity to teach children the properties of 3D shapes including cubes, pyramids and spheres. The activity requires children to make their thinking clear to themselves as well as others and to use discussion to explore and clarify their understanding.

The broader requirements for spoken language that this activity addresses are concerned with:

- asking relevant questions to extend their understanding and knowledge;
- giving well-structured descriptions.

In the Talk Box	A selection of different cubes, other cuboids, triangular- and square-based pyramids, cylinders and spheres. These could be a range of containers and packets, balls and mathematical shapes.
	This Talk Box should have a lid so that the shapes cannot be seen.

Maths talk

Tell the children that in the Talk Box are some solid (3D) shapes. Their task is to work out what shape is being described, without looking.

Choose one child to come up to the Talk Box and, without looking, choose and hold a shape without taking it out of the box. You could ask the child to wear a blindfold, or to keep their eyes shut. They should be aware that this is a kind of quiz and should not name the shape aloud. Now ask the child to share with the rest of the class some information that they can 'feel' about the shape. They might say things like:

It has a point at one end.

It is made of square faces.

You can roll it.

There are four triangles.

Two of the opposite ends are squares.

Ask the other children to talk to each other about what the shape could be.

Then choose someone to guess the name of the shape and give a reason why it might be that one.

Sharing maths points of view

Each group needs three different solid shapes. Ask the groups to talk together to find ways to sort the shapes so that they have two which are similar and one which is different. For example, if a group has a sphere, a cylinder and a cuboid, they might decide that the sphere and the cylinder are similar because they roll, and the cuboid does not.

When they have found one way to sort the shapes, ask the group to find a different way to sort them into two groups.

This time they might choose the cylinder and the cuboid as similar, as both have some flat surfaces, but the sphere is different because it does not.

Ask a group to show one way of sorting; the rest of the class can talk to each other to decide **why** the shapes have been sorted that way. They can then ask 'Have you sorted them like that because . . . ?'

Talk with the class about how giving careful descriptions about the shapes and being able to ask questions has helped them to work out each other's ideas about sorting the shapes.

Extension

Groups can think of 'What am I?' questions for guessing shapes. These can be written on paper in the shape of speech bubbles and put into the Talk Box. Groups can then take out a question, discuss what the answers might be, and match them with the correct shapes. For example:

I have a circle at each end. What am I?

I have six square faces. What am I?

I have four triangles and a square. What am I?

Geometry: Position and direction – patterns and sequences

This activity is about encouraging children to talk about how to order and arrange mathematical objects in patterns and sequences. It addresses the spoken language of maths: children must make their thinking clear to themselves as well as others, asking and answering questions to explore and clarify their understanding.

The broader requirements for spoken language that this activity addresses are concerned with:

- asking relevant questions to extend their understanding and knowledge;
- articulating and justifying answers;
- giving well-structured descriptions.

In the Talk Box	Examples of repeating patterns – fabric/wallpaper/wrapping paper samples, bead strings, plain shapes, Multilink or other construction material.
	Blank grids for each group to create and record patterns, a selection of counters, bricks, etc. for each group

Maths talk

Ask someone to select a sample of the repeating patterns. Ask the class to discuss what the pattern is: How does it repeat? Is it symmetrical? Are there examples of shapes turning? What would come next, before, above, below?

Sharing maths points of view

Provide each group with a pattern sample to talk about. You could provide Talking Points to start this discussion. Groups have to decide whether they agree, disagree or whether they are not sure.

Talking Points: Patterns

> The pattern is symmetrical.
>
> There is more than one shape.
>
> There are shapes that turn in the pattern.
>
> The next step in the pattern would be . . .

Ask groups to talk together to create their own sequences to make repeating patterns using counters or similar objects. Record patterns on the blank grids. These can then be swapped with other groups to identify and talk about the patterns, and used to ask questions as a class, putting new vocabulary to work.

Extensions

Use a graphics program to create and manipulate repeating patterns that follow particular rules: the children could be asked to work in groups to reverse direction, orientate from horizontal to vertical, create a number of repeats, explore what happens when colours are restricted or added, etc.

Ask the children to collect other examples of patterns and sequences from home, and make a display. The children can add statements and questions about their pattern.

Statistics

This is an activity to enable children to begin to sort and organise data, using objects, and to ask and answer questions about the number of objects by interpreting the information. The broader requirements for spoken language that this activity addresses are concerned with:

- asking relevant questions to extend their understanding and knowledge;
- articulating and justifying answers and opinions;
- considering and evaluating different viewpoints, attending to and building on the contributions of others.

In the Talk Box	One set of ten small items for each group: toy cars, model animals, items of doll's clothing, pictures or models of food, etc.

Maths talk

Use one set to talk about ways of sorting the items into groups. This sort could be according to colour, size, type, material and so on. Record the groups as a pictogram and discuss what it shows. For example: How many green vehicles? Which group has the most/fewest items in it? How could we find out how many items there are altogether?

Maths points of view

Now ask the groups to talk about how to sort their own sets of objects. You could give each group blank pictograms to record their decisions. Ask the groups to make up questions about their graphs. The graphs and questions can then be swapped with another group, and the children can talk together to work out the answers. This can be done on the IWB.

Extension

Ask groups to look at one another's work and say what is good about it. Ask children to select another set of objects and group them differently from any ideas they have seen. Ask children to say who has helped them to talk and listen.

Closing plenaries in mathematics sessions

Closing plenary sessions should focus first on the mathematics. Questions, answers and whole-class discussion provide opportunities to hear and use words which may never be heard in other contexts.

Plenary sessions should also focus on the children's perception of their talk with others. Children can nominate others who have used language clearly, explained well, listened attentively, asked a good question or are helpful to work with in a group. These talk skills can be introduced and practiced regularly through discussion focused on mathematics learning.

Chapter 6 — Spoken language in science

Talk Box activities use three important ideas from the KS1 Science National Curriculum: science words, what we think about science, and sharing science points of view.

Science words: 'The quality and variety of language that pupils hear and speak are key factors in developing their scientific vocabulary'.

What we think about science: 'Children must be assisted in making their thinking clear, both to themselves and others'.

Sharing science points of view: 'Teachers should ensure that children build secure foundations by using discussion to probe and remedy their misconceptions'.

Young children benefit from the experience of science in which they experience and observe things for themselves, are encouraged to be curious and ask questions, and begin to use simple scientific language to talk about what they have found out. Science provides invaluable opportunities for children to communicate their ideas in a variety of ways. Through science, children are necessarily involved in speculation, hypothesis, decision making and problem solving. Useful learning experiences can arise from the ways that you organise talk for learning in your classroom. For each child, learning in science starts from the opportunity to interact with materials, new vocabulary and one another's ideas in discussion.

In science Talk Box activities, children have opportunities to understand and learn as they look at things, talk about them using relevant vocabulary and listen to ideas – their own and those of their classmates. This mix of using memory, airing previous understandings and talking things through is a powerful way to approach new learning in any subject. In the next section, topics from the Science National Curriculum provide sample Talk Box activities and discussion points.

After exploration and discussion, children need you to support their learning by direct tuition of a **definitive scientific point of view**. This can be done through talk, by using resources such as books, simulations and video, or by demonstration and example, so that children accumulate a more robust evidence-based picture of how the world works, rather than relying on everyday guesswork.

Plants: Identify and name wild and garden plants including trees

Science words

Decide on between five and ten local plants that you are going to name. The choice of these will depend upon your location and season, so they cannot be specified here, but as an example:

(Trees) willow, sycamore, birch;

(Other) ivy, grass, geranium, primrose.

Ask the children to look at the plant material in the Talk Box and think of five words which will describe what they see. Use accurate vocabulary, for example:

In the Talk Box

Choose plants (bark, leaves, flowers, fruit, e.g. sycamore seeds, cones, etc.) which grow in and around your school, or ones which you can bring into the classroom

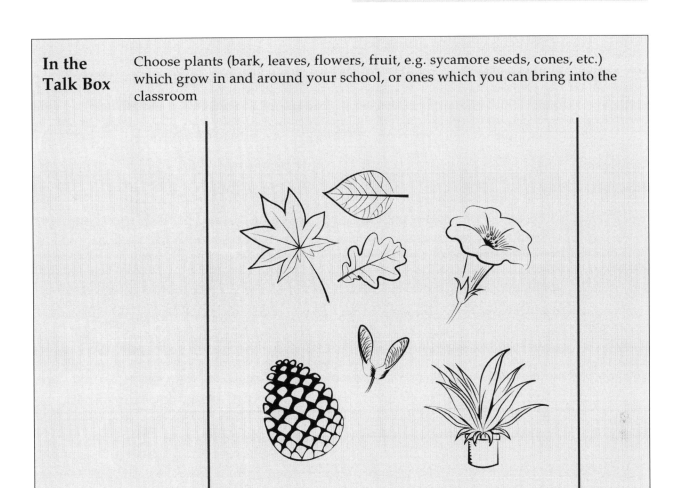

'dry', 'hard', 'knobbly', 'brown', 'pyramid' (fir cone);

'flat', 'green', 'wings', 'light', 'spreading' (sycamore seed);

'red', 'orange', 'thin', 'bright', 'stiff' (geranium flower).

Make these descriptions into a quiz to see if others can identify the plant material from what they hear.

Introduce the names of the plants you have chosen and ask children to practice naming the plants for one another. Ask children to think about why this is important.

Plant structure

In the Talk Box

Small boxes or plant pots, one per group, each containing five to ten items of plant material e.g. seeds, sprouted beans, bean roots or root vegetables; stems such as celery, flowers with stems, petals, leaves, grass, apples, fir cones, silk or plastic flowers, acorns

What we think about science

Ask groups to look at the plant material and think how they would sort the material into groups by looking at similarities and differences. Ask groups to share their ways of sorting. Now introduce the key vocabulary **'root'**, **'stem'**, **'leaf'**, **'flower'**, **'fruit'** – with examples – and ask the children to sort again. Ask which way of sorting the plants is the most useful.

Sharing science points of view

Ask groups to talk together to decide on the jobs of different parts of the plant. They should try to come up with two suggestions for each of **'root'**, **'stem'**, **'leaf'**, **'flower'**, **'fruit'**, with their reasons for the suggestions. Share ideas with the whole class and discuss with the class which suggestions seem most useful or helpful, or which are supported by good evidence or reasons. Complete this section by providing definitive information, e.g. leaves make sugar for the plant; roots take in water and provide anchorage; stems hold the leaves up to the light and transport water and sugar.

Plant structure and function

As seasons change, keep adding new plants to the list of plants the children now know. They need to know that people continue to learn such names throughout life. Teach the children exactly what each part of the plant is for, and provide opportunities to look at and use a range of plant material, e.g. wood, cork, bark, willow baskets, paper, card, root vegetables, cut flowers and fruit. Art activities can support this learning in science.

Animals: Vertebrate groups

In the Talk Box

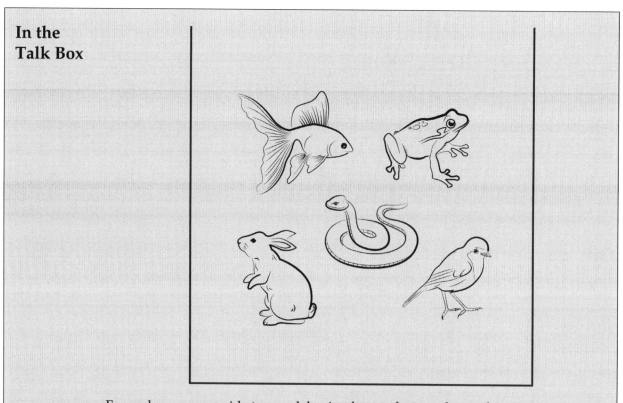

For each group, provide ten model animals, two from each vertebrate group, e.g. cat, rabbit, robin, penguin, goldfish, clownfish, crocodile, snake, frog, newt, etc.

Science words

Ask groups to look at their creatures, name them if possible, describe them and say which are pairs and why. Share ideas with the whole class.

Ensure that children know that all these creatures are animals, and why.

Look at a range of information that will help children to understand that vertebrate groups have distinctive skin covering, have their young in particular ways and have other characteristics which can help us to see that some are like each other, and so can usefully be grouped together.

Introduce the key vocabulary '**mammal**', '**bird**', '**fish**', '**reptile**', '**amphibian**' with lots of examples to look at, see, talk about and question. For example, the penguin does not have obvious feathers and swims like a seal, but lays hard eggs and belongs to the bird group.

Carnivores,
herbivores
and
omnivores

In the Talk Box	Picture or model of a child, dog, cat, rabbit, mouse, tins of food, cat food, dog food, baked beans, packets of seeds, cereal, grains, vegetables

Ask children to say which food would suit which creature and how they know.

Ask them to tell you about the teeth of each creature, and relate this to the food they have suggested.

Ask them to think about the sort of things creatures eat and their teeth shapes; draw out the link in terms of shape and function of teeth in relation to diet.

Science words

Introduce the key vocabulary '**carnivores**', '**herbivores**' and '**omnivores**' with examples.

What we think about science

Ask groups to decide what they think about why there are creatures that eat only plant material, why some eat other animals and why we as humans can do both.

You could use Talking Points as prompts for discussion.

Talking Points: What animals eat

The world would be much better if there were no carnivores.

Herbivores move slowly and have to sleep a lot.

It's easiest to be an omnivore because then you never run out of food.

Ask groups to share ideas with the whole class.

Summarise this topic by providing a clear picture of the way populations of creatures are balanced in terms of numbers, and their interdependence. Provide models or pictures of animal skulls which show their teeth (including dinosaurs) and ask groups to come to a reasoned decision about the diet of the animal.

Human body structure

Sharing science points of view

Find out what children already know about their own bodies and how they work. Starting with one of the body systems ask groups to draw or build a plasticine model of a person which shows the position and working of the bones of the skeleton, or the brain, nerves and senses.

Ask groups to make a model of the digestive system using junk materials.

Ask groups to monitor one another before and after two minutes' exercise, and account for the changes they notice in breathing, heart rate and how the person feels.

Choose key vocabulary ('heart', 'skin', 'blood', 'lungs', 'stomach', 'intestines', 'kidneys', 'brain', 'skeleton', 'skull') and help children to identify organs on a model or picture.

The senses

In the Talk Box	**Five animal pictures or toys** – e.g. rabbit/donkey (hearing), owl, toy animal, human baby, fox (sight), hedgehog (touch), snake (taste), bear/dog (smell)
	Ask children to name five 'senses mascots'. Describe and talk about the sense they are to represent. Ask children to think about how useful their own senses are.

Science words

Introduce the key vocabulary for senses; 'eyes', 'sight', 'ears', 'hearing', 'skin', 'touch', 'tongue', 'taste', 'nose', 'smell'. Ask groups to choose one of the senses mascots and make up a story where they use one particular sense to find something. Share the stories.

Sharing science points of view

Take one sense at a time and provide sets of material that will stimulate discussion for each group, as below, or arrange a 'circus' of activities. Ask children to be ready to describe what they did and what they noticed. Suggestions are:

Sight: blindfold (scarf); transparent coloured paper.

Ask children to help each other walk round the room while blindfolded, and to look at things through the coloured paper and describe what they see.

Hearing: earmuffs (scarf); different surfaces; ruler or wooden stick.

Ask children to describe the difference when wearing the earmuffs. Ask them to make up a tapping rhythm to share, with the surfaces and stick.

Taste: salty water, sugary water, pure water, straws, disposable cups.

Ask children to make up a test to see if others can tell the difference between the three sorts of 'water'; one drop only to be used.

Smell: garlic, perfume, peppermint oil.

Ask children to make up a test to see if others can guess the scents.

Touch: sandpaper, fur fabric, jelly, cooking oil, icy water, metal.

Ask children to make up a quiz in which they ask questions about how the materials feel for others to guess.

Everyday materials

In the Talk Box	A wide range of different types of paper

Ask groups to talk about what each type of paper is used for and why. Share ideas with the class.

What we think about science

Provide glue, scissors and an A3 sheet of paper for each group. Ask children to design and make a poster by cutting out 5 cm squares of each paper type and presenting them with information they want to share. Ask groups to decide how to undertake this practical work so that only one person is away from the work area (collecting paper samples, glue, etc.) at a time. As the posters are being made, ask groups to add information showing what they know about how paper is made, where it goes after it has been used, its properties, its cost and so on. Children's knowledge of such factual information is patchy but they will know enough to be able to contribute and to arouse curiosity in others.

Display the posters. Enable groups to research further information about, for example, types of paper, trees grown for paper, processing wood pulp, recycling paper and card.

Repeat with other materials, e.g. wood, metals, plastics, crystals.

Seasonal changes and day length

In the Talk Box	There are effective online simulations which show how the earth turns on its axis; how it is tipped at an angle to the vertical; how the earth moves around the sun and the influence of these movements on day length, seasons, and how much energy different areas of the earth receive. In this topic, the computer Talk Box provides the film, video clip or IWB software that you choose to use.

Sharing science points of view

Provide groups with a football/beach ball/safe battery lantern or light (sun) and a tennis ball (earth). For now, the moon can be left out of the picture! Ask groups to talk together and use the props to show – in this order:

1. the tilt of the earth on its axis;

2. the rotation of the earth on its axis;

3. day and night at one point on the earth (add in dawn and dusk if possible);

4. the movement of the earth around the sun;

5. spring, summer, autumn and winter at a point on the earth.

Observe groups to pick up misconceptions, and to find out which group can provide a good demonstration for the class, which group uses new vocabulary well and so on. Ensure, for example, that children realise that the earth is tilted on its axis of rotation, at about 23 degrees from the vertical (it does 'wobble' backwards and forwards but this change of direction of axis takes 26,000 years). It is the earth's permanent tilt that gives us our seasons over a year, as the surface of the earth receives sunlight over a smaller area (summer) and wider area (winter) as we move around the sun every 365 days. Ask everyone to listen to a definitive explanation, or watch a simulation, and ask questions. Find out if the children are interested in the earth and its place in space, the planets, the solar system, the space station and its astronauts; what do they already know, and what would they like to find out?

Ask groups to devise a drama in which they take the parts of the sun and earth. Add in the moon and its monthly spin around the earth, if possible, along with planets, a space station, rocket, astronaut, aliens, Clangers – anything the children want to use to help them retain their understanding of day and night and seasons, and which will foster their continuing curiosity.

What can we say is 'Living', 'Dead', or has 'Never been alive'

In the Talk Box	Pot plant, cut flowers or leaves, wood, paper, metal, stone

Bring out these things and ask children to look at them and explain to one another which category they belong to – 'Living', 'Dead', 'Never been alive'.

Ask groups to devise a definition for 'living'.

Look at the idea of 'fire' – use pictures or film. Fire moves, uses oxygen, can grow and reproduce by sparks; it behaves like a living thing. What do groups think and why?

Ask children to consider the idea of growing and developing as a building process in which simple materials are used to make complex body structures: this is what true living things do.

A magical building that can create itself out of bricks, mortar, glass, plastic, water, pipes, electrical cables and so on serves as a useful analogy. Similarly, a tree can make itself with the addition of just water, carbon dioxide and sunshine, whereas a fire cannot create such structure.

It's best to use simple examples for this topic because some materials can be confusing; hair, feathers and wool can be considered as 'never been alive'; plastics, petrol and other liquids are made from oil which is plant material and has been alive; chalk and limestone rocks are made from seashells, but was this protective covering ever alive? Once the basic concept of living, dead, never been alive, is secure children certainly can have these discussions.

Materials

In the Talk Box	One small plant pot, box or disposable cup for each group, containing about ten items made from a range of materials: Lolly stick, pencil, plastic and metal spoons, rubber, pencil sharpener, fridge or other magnet, plastic and paper cup, glass beads or marbles, silk flower, piece of Lego, counter, small sample of felt/fabric/carpet/velvet/lace/ribbon/wool, elastic band, plastic and 'real' cork, two different coloured coins, sandpaper/electric wire/spanner/bottle of water, etc.

Science words

Ask children to talk about what the things are for, what they are made of, and why they are made of this material. Ask each group to prepare to tell the class this information about an item of their choice. Foster accurate vocabulary such as 'metal', 'cotton', 'plastic', 'strong', 'flexible', 'transparent', 'colourful', 'rigid', etc.

Children can look around the room and choose any item to analyse – what is it made of, and why? Can other materials be used? What other materials have been used in the past?

Sharing science points of view

Explain and demonstrate some key differences between metals and non-metals in terms of their properties, showing lots of examples.

Metals can be shiny, hard, heavy for their size and may be flexible or strong.

Non-metals can be shiny or not, tend to be light for their size and may be rigid, strong, flexible or elastic.

Ask groups to design something, drawing it and specifying the materials they might use and why – for example, a toy for a younger child, a pet cage, a watering can, a new coin, a plant pot, a phone case, gloves. Ask groups to share their ideas with the class, and ask the class to provide positive feedback on the materials that have been suggested.

Exercise

In the Talk Box	Skipping rope, small and large ball, hoop, cone, whistle, trainers, t-shirt, stopwatch, water bottle, towel, apple, bat or racquet, and so on

Science words

Ask children to name and describe the objects in the Talk Box, and to say how they help us to exercise. Ask children to discuss these Talking Points and to prepare a response to one of them to share with the class.

Talking Points: Exercise

Exercise and sport are the same thing.

Everyone needs some exercise every day.

Exercise is expensive.

What we think about science

Ask groups to select one of the Talk Box items, and use it to make up a short story about someone who doesn't like exercise – these can be oral stories or cartoons. Ask groups to share their stories and come up with a sentence or 'slogan' to encourage people to take regular exercise.

Closing plenaries in science sessions

Closing plenary sessions should focus first on the science. Questions, answers and whole-class discussion are an invaluable opportunities to hear and use words that may never be heard in other contexts.

Plenary sessions should also focus on the children's perception of their talk with others. Children can nominate others who have used language clearly, explained well, listened attentively, asked a good question or are helpful to work with in a group. These talk skills can be introduced and practiced regularly through discussion focused on science learning.

Chapter 7

Talk in English

A focus on talking about story and poems. Children's talk, reading and writing interlinked.

Children learn to talk in school

Children develop oral language by listening to others and creatively copying and using what they hear to form their own words for their own purposes. Once a child can talk, their thoughts are shaped by language, and language shapes how they express their thoughts. There are clear and obvious links between talking and thinking, and talking and reading. The sounds of speech are encapsulated in written words; the symbols of the English language represent sounds. Reading is what happens when sounds are put back into texts, so that even silent reading may involve 'saying' words to ourselves. In effect, we literally or metaphorically breathe life into written words by reading them, aloud or silently. Thus reading and speaking are inextricably linked, and the capacity to read is profoundly dependent on the capacity to speak and listen.

For children with good language skills, reading may be readily learned. For children whose speech is not so well developed, who cannot focus on what they hear or who have heard very little spoken language, reading is made more difficult. In school, we teach reading very carefully, knowing that it is the key to educational success and personal achievement. We teach collectively but children learn to read individually, each one making the creative and imaginative leaps that help them to decode text, make meaning from print and add in the intonation and liveliness that good reading requires. Children mainly learn to read in school, and are taught assiduously by means of phonics, story, poetry, rhyme, rhythm, look and say, whole book teaching, and through methods based on individual language experience, or using carefully contextualised texts which have high interest value – every child is carefully taught to read, for very good reasons.

Children also learn to speak individually, but learning of spoken language is often informal, casual or oblique: it may not be taught directly. Children learn to talk in school, but they are rarely taught how talk works with the same priority as that given to the teaching of reading. The direct teaching of speaking and listening is, for many children, the only opportunity to get to grips with the complexities of oral language use, to be shown what words can do, to be accorded insight into the ways people work with words to communicate, or to accumulate a working vocabulary in a range of topics. For every child, the chance to be taught to listen, ask questions, ask for and give reasons, explain, elaborate, negotiate, summarise and present hypothetical or more established ideas must be seen as an essential element of their early education – but carefully planned tuition in such skills, progressing through the school years, is very unusual. The essential aims of such teaching are to ensure that every child is provided with the skills and understanding needed in order to become an articulate speaker, an active listener and, through these capacities, a fluent reader and thoughtful writer.

Children learn to talk in school – if they can. Whether they like talking, whether anyone ever listens to them or examines their thoughts aloud with them, has immediate influence on their learning of how to talk effectively. Children's starting vocabulary and their ability to join in with a group that is talking, taking turns and accepting challenge without feeling personally threatened, may stand them in good stead as learners of talk, or may be the reasons why they never learn. In addition, children's awareness of the value of talk for their own thinking and that of others affects how readily they contribute and gain from talk. Unless awareness is raised, a child may never understand the link between talking and thinking, and the value of talk with others for their own individual development. It is extremely unfortunate to have to say that actually the title of this section is inaccurate, and should instead read, 'Only some children learn to talk in school' – those who do already can. A neglect of the teaching of oracy is a recipe for continuing inequality and consolidating disadvantage. Teachers know this, but the single most important influence preventing the teaching of speaking and listening is the drive for *evidence*. Teachers must teach things that produce immediate, written evidence which can be marked according to criteria that are measureable such as spelling, grammar, punctuation and mathematical knowledge. Instead of helping every child towards oral language competence, teachers are compelled to teach arcane and divisive programmes that are used to measure, grade and demoralise them.

Children need to talk if they are to read well; they need to talk and read to stimulate thinking, and they need to think for themselves in order to write creatively and effectively.

Talking about stories and poems

This chapter takes two stories – the traditional tale *Puss in Boots* and the wonderful picture story *The Scarecrow's Hat* by Ken Brown, and provides a talk-focused approach to reading and writing. We also look at a poem as an example. We provide Talk Box activities which incorporate these important ideas from the KS1 English National Curriculum, focusing on Writing:

Preparing to write: children prepare by saying what they are going to write about, thinking aloud as they collect ideas.

Developing positive attitudes towards writing through drawing on experiences both real and fictional, and by planning together to write in a range of 'real' contexts for different purposes.

A collaborative approach to this organising of ideas before and during the process of writing enables children to apply their developing speaking and listening skills. Talk Box activities in this section are designed to support this work. Activities are not presented as 'lesson plans' but outlines for you to modify. Learning arises from the opportunity to interact with materials, vocabulary and one another's ideas in discussion.

Bringing a story to life through talk

Before reading

1. Ask the children to talk in their groups to name the items and say what they are used for, what materials they are made from and why, and if they are familiar with the items.

2. Introduce the characters Scarecrow and Chicken by showing the cover picture. Ask groups to decide what they can say about these two – Are they friends? Are they happy or sad? What sort of place do they live in? and so on.

In the Talk Box

The Scarecrow's Hat by Ken Brown

A hat, a walking stick (mountain walking or other), a length of ribbon, some wool or a woollen item, a pair of glasses, a blanket and some feathers

3. Ask the children to think about their Ground Rules for Talk. The focus of this talk for reading activity is for each child to give reasons, to ask for reasons and see if the reasons can help them to change their mind or feel surer of their own ideas.

   Explain and model *asking for and giving reasons*. One way to do this is to ask your TA to take part in a role play where you both give very different reasons for the questions about Chicken and Scarecrow (Activity 2), and then talk together to negotiate some sort of compromise. Ask children to comment on the quality of your discussion.

   Ask groups to discuss the Talking Points, focusing on reasoning and ensuring everyone is asked to contribute. This discussion is not about the plot of the story, but issues associated with the story.

Talking Points: *The Scarecrow's Hat*

Scarecrows are very rare.

You shouldn't swap things, you should pay for things.

We all have things that might help other people.

4. Learning a sentence:

   'Now Chicken didn't have a *walking stick*, but she knew someone who did'.

   This is the book's refrain; the words in italics change. Ask children to read and learn this sentence. Look carefully at these words:

   'hat', **'walking stick'**, **'ribbon'**, **'wool'**, **'pair of glasses'**, **'blanket'**, **'feathers'**.

   Help children to learn to read these words and the whole sentence. When reading the whole book later, make sure that less secure readers are asked to read this sentence for the group or the class.

5. **Prepare to read the book** with the children by choosing eight children to be characters; they are going to be Scarecrow, Chicken, Badger, Jackdaw, Sheep, Owl, Donkey and Duck. Show pictures of the creatures and find out what children know about them. Give each character a big name label if you wish.

   Give the items from the Talk Box to the appropriate character, so at the start of the story, Chicken has the feathers, Donkey has the blanket, Owl has the glasses and so on – Scarecrow should be wearing the hat.

Reading

Now read the story. You can use the IWB to show the text and ask children to join in the refrain, or choose children to help with the reading. When Donkey agrees to swap the blanket for feathers, ask Chicken to give his/her feathers to Donkey in exchange for the blanket. Chicken will then take the blanket to Owl and exchange it for the pair of glasses, then the pair of glasses to Sheep . . . and so on (this is highly unlikely to go right first time!). Read the story two or three times so that everyone can be a character.

After reading

1. Focus vocabulary, phonic and look/say work on these words:

   'chicken', 'jackdaw', 'owl', 'sheep', 'donkey', 'duck', 'badger', 'ribbon', 'glasses', 'hat', 'feathers', 'wool blanket', 'straw', 'stone', 'ledge', 'pair', 'awake', 'buzzing', 'tail', 'nice', 'replied'.

2. Ask groups to talk together to make up an oral version of this story with themselves in it, swapping things like Lego, computer games, cars, hairbands, pencils, books, soft toys and so on.

3. Ask groups to choose their favourite character and carry out some research to find out as much as they can, to share with the class. Decide on a format for presentation. This might be a homework task.

4. Ask groups to look at the watercolour illustrations in the original book and decide on a page to illustrate in another medium.

Writing

1. Ask groups to talk together to choose a character, then decide on and write sentences that tell that character's story.

2. Ask groups to talk together and decide what they like and dislike about the text and illustrations in this book. Write or present a book review.

3. Ask groups to take one character and write a thank-you letter to Chicken describing their new item and saying why they are pleased with it; or ask the class to write a letter from Chicken to her sister describing how she acquired the hat for her nest.

4. Ask children to find out as much as they can about their favourite animal in the book, and write an information page or compile a presentation that they can talk through for the class.

The following activities use the traditional story *Puss in Boots* as the context for talking and writing. Activities can be adapted to work with other stories that the children might be familiar with, or that you might prefer.

Puss in Boots

In the Talk Box

Choose a version of the story that you like for the Talk Box. There are lots of versions in print, on film and on YouTube. A print version has some advantages, not least the idea of reading together.

Prepare to read the story

Display and teach the names of the characters and scenes:

Characters: Miller's Son, Puss in Boots, King, Ogre, Princess, Marquis of Carabas.

Scenes: river, meadow, castle.

Read and talk about the story.

After reading

1. **A play:** Ask groups to animate or make up a freeze-frame of a scene, or add extra characters or scenes. Dramatise the story to share with other classes.

2. **Class cats:** Find out about cats belonging to children in the class, in the school and adults at the school. Ask families to bring in or send photos. Discuss which cat

would best suit the role of Puss in Boots. Organise hustings and a vote. Create a story in which all the cats appear as characters.

3. **Versions:** Collect a range of print and digital versions of the story. Enable groups to access these and make comparisons, deciding which they prefer and why.

Writing: Talking about instructions – how to catch a rabbit

This activity focuses on discussion about writing instructions. The children discuss what they are going to write about, and sequence their instructions in short sentences, supported by illustrations if they wish. Teaching speaking and listening involves modelling and describing how to provide well-structured explanations and participate in a focused conversation with their group.

In the traditional version of *Puss in Boots*, the Master Cat decides to catch various animals as gifts to please the King: one of these is a rabbit. This adventure is used as the context for the Talk Box activity.

In the Talk Box

Examples of different types of instructions, for example a recipe, rules for a game, a plan of how to build a model, etc.

For each group, a set of pictures and/or items that may or may not be useful to help the Master Cat to catch a rabbit: lettuce, rope, ladder, box, carrot, cheese, torch, etc.

Start by re-reading the story together, and drawing attention to the part of the story where Puss catches a rabbit to give to the King. Perhaps you could ask the children to role play this section of the story.

Introduce the idea of instructions by talking about how we explain how to do something. You could use the examples of instructions in the Talk Box to illustrate this. How do we know how to play a game? Make a cake? Build a model? Draw attention to the way that pictures and words can sometimes be used together to make the meaning clear. Talk about the language used to ensure instructions are sequential (e.g. 'first', 'next', 'finally'), the use of imperative verbs (e.g. 'put', 'chop', 'make') and the ways instructions are ordered or numbered (e.g. 'ingredients', 'method').

Sharing ideas

Ask each group to use the set of pictures and objects in the Talk Box to decide a plan for catching a rabbit (alive!): What would they use and why? How would the plan work? After they have agreed what they will use and devised a plan, they could work together to record this as a set of instructions: 'How to catch a rabbit'. Perhaps this could be a drawing that they label, or a set of written instructions.

Discuss how it felt to share ideas before writing. Did it help everyone to think about what to write and how to write it? Ask individuals for examples of good listening and sharing of ideas.

Follow-up activities

These could include:

trying to follow incomplete instructions and writing the missing parts;

writing a set of instructions to carry out a simple task and then testing these by asking other children, or people at home, to follow them carefully;

cross-curricular links with maths (using a programmable robot to follow a simple route) and geography (giving instructions to follow a simple route on a map or plan).

Talking and writing about the characters in the story: How are they feeling?

This activity is designed to encourage discussion of ideas about emotions before composing a collaborative piece of writing. Sentences are constructed orally before being recorded. This provides opportunities to use spoken language to explore ideas and express feelings, as well as listening to and building on other people's contributions.

In the Talk Box

A picture of each character

A story board showing the different scenes in the story.

An example of these scenes:

The miller's son is given only a cat.

The cat says he will help if he has boots and a bag.

The cat gives gifts to the king.

The cat tricks the king into helping his master and believing that he is rich.

The cat's master and the princess fall in love.

The cat meets the ogre and tricks him in order to get his castle for his master.

The princess and the cat's master marry and everyone lives happily ever after.

After re-reading the story, ask the class to collect words that might describe different emotions or feelings, and write each of these on a separate card.

Sharing ideas

Each group considers one character chosen from the Talk Box. Ask them to use the storyboard and talk together to decide how that character might be feeling at the different points of the story. Using the words on the feelings cards as a guide, each member of the group then helps to write a sentence for part of the story and explains why the character felt that way. Finally, they could consider evidence from the story to agree on when the character felt happiest/most frightened/angry, and so on.

Further activities

Ask groups to work together to compile a living graph showing all the characters and how their emotions changed throughout the story.

Add sentences to pictures of the characters, recording how they were feeling and why at particular points of the story. Talk together to decide how this is different for each character depending on their point of view.

Cross-curricular activities

PSHE: Circle time activities about feelings. What happens to make feelings change in the story, and in life? Do feelings always change?

History: Discuss and describe different points of view about people and events.

Considering points of view: Thinking about Puss and the Ogre

In this activity children are encouraged to consider part of the story from different perspectives, imagining what two characters might be thinking. This enables children to share their ideas and opinions, and compose writing orally before recording it. The spoken language focuses on participation in discussion through speculation and exploration of ideas.

In the Talk Box

Pictures or toys to represent the cat and the ogre.

Sets of Talking Points, for example:

Talking Points: Puss and the Ogre

The ogre is surprised to have an unexpected visitor.

The cat is very brave to ask to speak to the ogre.

The ogre is clever because he can change into different creatures.

The ogre is easily tricked so is really a bit silly.

The cat is foolish as the ogre could easily eat him.

It must have been terrifying for the cat when the ogre became a lion.

It was very cunning of the cat to persuade the ogre to change into a mouse.

Begin by re-telling the story with the class, concentrating on the meeting between the cat and the ogre. Ask volunteers to role play this meeting and 'freeze-frame' it at certain points, then ask the class to talk together to say how each character might be feeling and what they might be thinking at these points. Encourage children to give reasons or explanations for their answers.

Sharing ideas

Ask the talk groups to discuss the Talking Points and decide how the ogre and the cat are feeling and what they are thinking during their meeting.

Next, ask groups to imagine that they are the cat. What would they do and say to persuade the ogre to change into a mouse? When the group has agreed, record this joint idea in a speech bubble. What might the ogre be thinking? Again, record in a similar way.

Further activities

Ask groups to collaborate to make a short cartoon-style story strip to record the whole encounter. Each group could make one part, then these could be copied and used as a sequencing activity.

Cross-curricular activities

PSHE: Look at pictures of faces representing different emotions and discuss what emotions are recognisable. Record and display words to describe the emotion around the face picture.

Music: Listen to a selection of different short pieces or excerpts. Ask children to talk together to share their reactions, and say what emotions the music might convey. Record these ideas on music paper.

What happened next?

This activity enables groups to think imaginatively, sharing their ideas and composing a short piece orally before recording it. The spoken language focuses on articulating and justifying opinions and exploring ideas, as well as using appropriate language for persuasion.

In the Talk Box	Sets of objects and/or pictures of things that the cat might or might not like as rewards Letter templates for each group/child

Begin this activity with the whole class by focusing on the final part of the story: Is the cat the hero? Why? Do you think he is given the right reward for all his efforts?

Sharing ideas

Ask the groups to look at the objects and pictures and discuss which things they think the cat might like to ask for as a reward. Can they agree on a favourite? When they have reached a conclusion, decide together what they might say in a short letter to the Marquis to ask for the chosen reward. Use the letter template to record this either as a group or individually, if appropriate.

Further activities

Look together at other letters in stories – for example *The Jolly Postman*. Talk about what different kinds of letters are used for.

Imagine the cat has gone on holiday as his reward. Talk together about what he might write in his postcard to the Marquis.

Ask groups to discuss and write a letter from the Marquis to his brothers, telling them what happened, asking them to the wedding and asking them to keep his secret. Groups can write the replies too.

Extension activities for talk fluency

1. **Boots:** Ask children to bring in boots – any kind. Ask groups to talk about, draw and describe the boots, saying what they are made of and in what setting they would be most useful. Ask groups to design boots for a cat who does not want to walk in the mud, for the Princess or King, or to create their own welly boot design and write a description.

2. **More boots:** Puss in the traditional story does not seem to use the boots for anything in particular. Ask groups to talk about why the boots are important, and write an extra scene in which the boots are used in some way.

3. **Cats:** Ask groups to decide on their favourite of the class cats and draw and describe its appearance, personality, likes and dislikes, with reasons for their decision.

   Ask groups to find out about a cat of their choice – domestic or large cat – and prepare a presentation or fact sheet about it to share.

   Make and play a Top Trumps cat game.

4. **Email:** Allocate a character to each group, e.g. Puss in Boots, Marquis of Carabas, Princess, Ogre, King. Set up an email conversation in which they have to ask questions to find out more about one another, and reply to questions asked.

5. **Comparison review:** Ask groups to discuss and decide on their favourite version of the story, and write a review recommending it to younger children and saying why they like it best.

6. **Evaluate:** Ask groups to talk about their discussion groups and provide positive feedback on oracy by saying who was good to work with and why; who listened or shared ideas well who was good at making suggestions, explaining and describing and so on. You can have badges to distribute for stars in each category, or ensure that every child has heard a positive comment about the way they have talked to others during the *Puss in Boots* work.

Talk about a poem

The poem *Cat's Eyes* is used as a basis for discussion and creativity. You will have favourite and important poems you would like to share with your class and can adapt these talk-focused activities.

Cat's Eyes

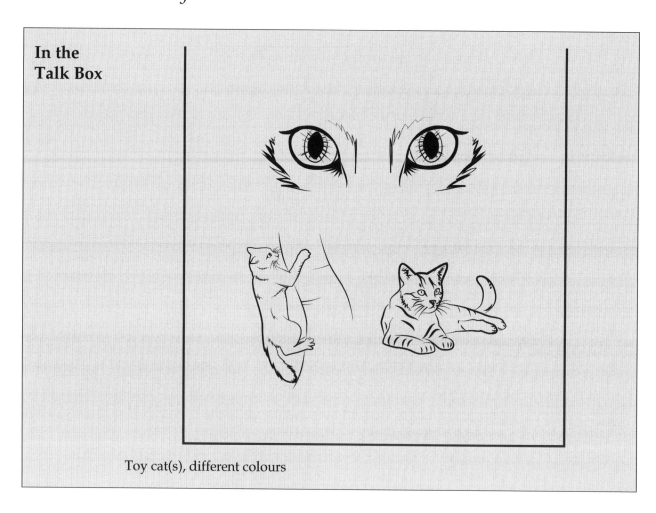

In the Talk Box

Toy cat(s), different colours

Show the cats and ask children to tell each other what they know about cats.

Share this information by asking children to say what a group mate has told them.

Read the poem in a whole-class setting, pausing before the rhyme to allow children time to predict it.

Cat's Eyes

If you see a black cat
It's your lucky day,

If you see a tortoiseshell
You can go out to play.

If you see an orange cat
The weather will be fine,

If you see a stripy cat
You have to count to nine.

If you see a climbing cat
It's off to see the view,

If you see cats' eyes on the road
They're looking out for you.

Activities

Provide copies of the poem for the children to read together.

1. Look at the pattern of the poem, the repetition of 'If you see . . .' and the rhyme scheme;

2. Check that the children understand the colloquial phrase 'looking out for you';

3. Ask groups to write another stanza. You can offer starters, for example:

   If you see a cat's claws; If you see a sleeping cat

   Or alter it slightly . . . If you stroke a furry cat / If you feed a hungry cat . . .;

4. Research the cats' eyes that we see on roads; how they work, when they were first used, where and how they are used, different colours of cats' eyes at junctions and so on;

5. Provide electronic copies of the poem and ask the groups to illustrate or annotate their copy, adding any extra stanzas they have written;

6. Ask groups to write a 'Cat Sense' poem, a cat shape poem or acrostic simply using the word 'cat' or a cat's name. Cats offer the chance to write about contrasts, e.g. soft fur/sharp claws, independent/friendly, sleepy/alert;

7. Look at other poems about cats – there are many.

Chapter 8   Talk Box activities across the curriculum

Teaching specific types of talk that can enhance learning in particular subjects, including vocabulary work.

In this chapter, there are examples of Talk Box activities that you can adapt for your class across a range of curriculum subjects including IT, history, geography, PSHE, art and music. Children's learning in particular subjects is enhanced through the teaching of types of talk specific to that area of the curriculum. The activities incorporate specialised vocabulary and particular forms of discussion-based enquiry that are relevant to a subject.

IT: Talk Box and computers

Children are familiar with many sorts of electronic devices that can be considered as 'Talk Boxes' for the purposes of stimulating useful discussion. Many of the activities throughout the *Talk Box* book benefit from integrating technology that has the useful capacity to motivate, in addition to finding and saving information and ideas for presentation, recording talk and role plays, and of course to carry out their more mundane functions such as printing and copying. School provision varies, and changes are so rapid that it seems best not to be specific, but to share some general principles for effective educational use of these versatile machines.

Computers and classroom talk

The combination of computers, children's minds and their spoken language is extremely powerful. We don't need to teach children how to use computer games, but we do need to teach them how to use talk to get the best out of educational software. There is nothing more frustrating than watching children clicking thoughtlessly and casually when slowing down and reading, thinking and engaging with ideas would really help them to learn. Once a child is familiar with how to use spreadsheets, word processors, communication links, software for presentation or a particular teaching and learning programme, they are ready to use IT for learning in curriculum areas and for learning how to learn with one another. There are some key aspects of a classroom context that really help children to understand why and how to use computers. These suggestions are worth considering to help children get the most out of the software, their own ideas and the collaboration of their classmates.

Talk and computers: What contexts support learning?

1. **Exploratory Talk.** Children working in groups need to know how to discuss their ideas with one another using Exploratory Talk. The alternative is that they compete, disputing one another's suggestions with no reasons given, or that they are casually agreeable but disengaged. If one child dominates the proceedings, then they may as well be working on their own. If a child cannot contribute orally because they are handicapped by their social setting, they are in effect not part of the group at all. If you want children to work constructively in groups, or if you want to use IT to help children learn how and why to take part in teamwork, then teaching them how to use the tool of Exploratory Talk is essential.

   In a nutshell, if a child cannot discuss their ideas effectively with the child seated next to them, they are unlikely to be able to do so online with a child halfway around the world.

2. **Beat the clock.** Racing against the clock or competing within a time limit is fine for some activities, but not if you want children to discuss their ideas or step back to make evidence-based or reasoned decisions. Switch the clock off or ensure that children know that their talk and thinking is the focus for their time at the computer. Whizzing through a game is fun, but there are other ways to use computers and children need help to realise this.

3. **Equality.** Your class will have a range of IT provision at home and therefore be 'mixed ability' when it comes to technical skills and understanding. This variety of expertise provides opportunities for every child to teach and learn. They will have to be taught to understand that sharing knowledge does not dilute it, but consolidates and extends it. It's when we put what we know to use in conversation that we find the limits and depths of our understanding, and draw together what may have been disparate ideas to see the bigger picture. Use your class experts to teach others and get them up to speed. Asking and answering questions, and teaching and learning, are life skills the 'expert' and the 'novice' both need to learn. Arrange tutorials or demonstrations where the knowledge of 'how it works' or 'how to do it' is shared, so that the whole class moves towards joint understanding and competence in computer skills. Only once they are freed from the anxieties of perceiving themselves as 'better' or 'worse' at the mechanics of the enterprise can children support one another's learning.

4. **Shared expectations.** Communication over distance and time is a wonderful thing. Planning is essential – children need to reflect on and share what they expect from one another, evaluate together and think of next steps based on the experience of what has been achieved.

5. **Time planning.** A plan for learning that involves using computers must involve the ring-fencing of some **time** that is genuinely freed up from other demands. For example, the interactive whiteboard (IWB) offers teachers and children so many ways to work and learn. Planning can help to ensure that the IWB is a truly shared resource, 'owned' by every child as well as the teacher, and that creative findings and outcomes are discussed and evaluated. Using IT takes time in planning, in activity and in evaluation. Time is of the essence in primary classrooms. Planning for oral starter and closing plenary sessions enables you to highlight creativity and generates those magic moments when learning becomes evident, and new and interesting questions arise. Planning talk time before, during and after computer use can make all the difference.

Your school will have evolved varied ways of working with its computers. It is worth sharing expertise amongst your near colleagues. Perhaps you might start by looking at the Talk Box list of five general points with your colleagues to see what you would add, alter or prioritise.

IT activity:
Talk about
games

In the **Talk Box**	A computer game or character from a game

Group talk

Ask the group to take it in turn to share descriptions of their favourite game. Provide a list of prompts to ensure that the discussions stay on track, for example:

- your favourite game – reasons for this and rules for using the game;
- rules for using devices at home and reasons for home rules;
- characters in the game – what they do and why;
- who you play with and what you enjoy about playing the game in company.

It is useful for children to compare their ideas and experiences with their peers, and to consider that their ideas of what might be 'usual' or 'normal' are actually individual, and may not be 'usual' at all.

Talk Box and history

One of the aims of the history curriculum is to understand continuity and change over time, enabling children to understand contrasts and make connections, to speculate, ask questions and to write accounts.

History activity: Communicate!

This activity asks children to examine how communication has changed within living memory, looking at similarities and differences between methods of communication today and those used in the past. It develops the concepts of 'old' and 'new', and encourages children to think about the changes that have occurred during their own lives and during those of the adults they know.

In the Talk Box

Collections of different objects used for communication in the past and present day, for example, sets of the following items for each group:

A fountain pen and ink, biro, stationery for letter writing with examples of both handwritten and printed letters, postcards, birthday cards and Christmas cards, printouts of emails, texts, tweets, blogs and so on

Examples or pictures of telephones from both past and present, including, for example, a photograph of a telephone box and mobile phones

Pictures of computers, laptops, iPads, smartphones, a typewriter, tablets, a fax machine, etc.

Begin by talking with the class about ways of staying in touch and talking with other people when you are not together; point out that this is something that people have always needed to do. Ask how they stay in touch with family and friends who do not live nearby – is this the same for the adults they know? Look together at an example from each of the sets of objects in the Talk Box. How do these help us to stay in touch? Which ones might we use now?

Sharing ideas

Allocate a set of the communication objects or pictures from the Talk Box to each group, asking them to talk together and agree how to arrange the items in order from oldest to newest. Are there useful questions that they could ask? For example, 'Does someone in my family have one now?' 'Have you used one of these?'

After the groups have agreed on a way to arrange the items, discuss whether there were any that were harder to place, and try to work out where they might fit – there may not be an exact placing. Introduce the idea of continuity and change over time. For example, versions of a pen have been used for writing for a long time, but their form and the materials used to make them have altered considerably.

Ask groups to say how the items are similar, and in what ways they are different.

The groups can then discuss a way to record their timeline for each item; perhaps they could take photographs and label these if they are using objects, or arrange them on a blank timeline? Ask groups to compare their own timelines with those of other groups. Do they agree with how they have been arranged? What questions could they ask one another?

Ensure that there is time to discuss the role of group talk in coming to decisions about the timelines, and in presenting information for the rest of the class.

Extension activities

1. Children can study other everyday things in the same way. Other items could be sorted and ordered, for example toys and games or household items (pictures of irons, washing machines, devices for listening to music, etc.).

2. Ask the children to consider what methods of communication might be developed in the future. They could design an item that they think is an improvement on current similar items. In what ways is their version similar to what we have now, and what is different?

3. Ask children to interview teachers, other adults, parents and grandparents or other family members about the tools they had for communication during their lifetime. What are the similarities and differences? You can link this activity with other topics, for example: more general consideration of the need to communicate; advantages of instant communication; staying safe online; useful ways of using spoken language and written language.

Talk Box and PSHE	Talk, thoughts, learning, feelings, ideas – PSHE offers wonderful contexts for discussion. We offer two activity ideas here. An important precursor is to ensure that children know how to engage one another in Exploratory Talk, and that there is always time to ask for positive feedback for individuals about the quality of spoken language after discussion sessions.
PSHE activity 1: Mirrors	In this activity, mirrors are used as a starting point for more abstract discussion of 'reflection' as a metaphor for thinking.

In the Talk Box

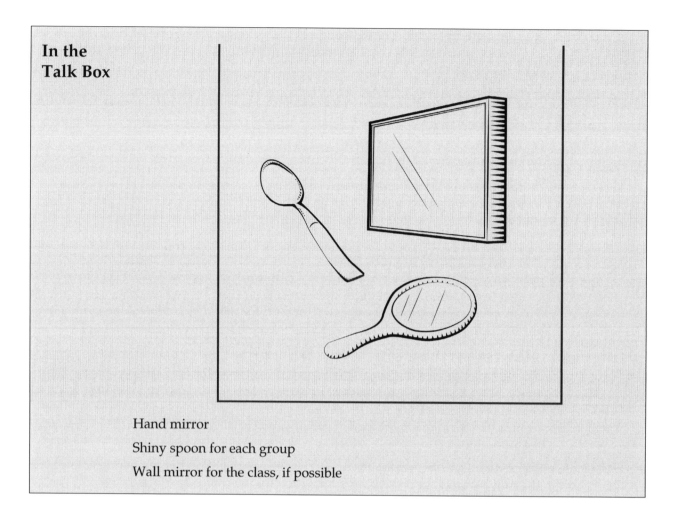

Hand mirror

Shiny spoon for each group

Wall mirror for the class, if possible

Activity

Ask the children to look at the mirrors and describe to each other how they work. Listen for use of specialised vocabulary such as 'reflection'. Ask groups to say where they think the reflection actually is; if it is inverted, symmetrical, distorted, clear, cloudy, and perhaps why. Ask groups to discuss their ideas and make up two questions about how mirrors work that they would like to ask the rest of the class. Alternatively, ask groups to use the mirrors to look at reflections of a toy, making up and answering questions about the toy and its image in the mirror. Make up a story conversation between the toy and the toy that appears in the mirror, perhaps involving a question-and-answer sequence.

Take each group in turn and encourage them to ask their 'mirror' questions and choose a classmate to answer. Bring into the conversation the idea that 'reflection' can also mean 'thinking'. We reflect on things by considering them carefully before saying anything or doing anything. The mirror holds images; similarly, the mind holds words and images for us to think about. Reflection might involve 'talking to yourself' or might be much more abstract than words allow. Ask children for their experiences of reflecting on events, decisions or aspects of their lives. If this is a very unfamiliar idea for the class, provide a context for reflection, for example ask children to think for a few minutes about some 'big ideas' such as:

Talking Points: Reflecting on today

Today we are lucky to be so healthy and well fed.

The place we live in is good, and better than a lot of children's home areas.

We have people who are helping us while we grow up.

My friends are important and know that I value them.

I am trying hard at school today.

Something I am looking forward to is . . .

Today I know I am good at . . .

Today I would like to learn about . . .

Reflections about ourselves

Ask groups to talk about some or all of these ideas:

Talking Points: Reflections in mirrors

I am not the same in the mirror.

A reflection is made of light.

Looking in a mirror is the same as looking at a friend.

I like mirrors.

I'm surprised by my reflection sometimes.

A reflection and a photograph are very similar.

I never look in a mirror.

After discussion, ask groups to share their thoughts.

If you think this is appropriate for your class, ask the children to think quietly and on their own (use the word reflect) for a few minutes, about 'Today'. Remind them that reflection involves using their memory. Ask them to think about an idea such as:

'I can reflect on what I have learned in school today'.

'I often reflect on things that have gone well, or gone wrong'.

'I can reflect on things I am grateful for'.

'I can reflect on the help I am given at school'.

'I can reflect on things I would like to change'.

'I can reflect on what sort of person I want to grow up to be'.

'I can reflect on what a friend is'.

Extension activity

Encourage the children to look around for other reflective surfaces such as polished metal, windows (when it's dark outside), puddles and shiny things.

PSHE activity 2: A person is a box

In this activity, children reflect on the idea of individual experience and think of ways to communicate feelings and ideas. Start by acknowledging that, despite our human ability to communicate through talk, people are individuals and we each experience and feel things separately.

It can be useful for children to consider themselves as a separate 'box': as people, they are sensitive, responsive and able to communicate; they can be hurt by others, physically or by words or deeds; they can explain their thoughts, ideas and feelings; and they can listen to others talking.

Talk to the children about their individuality and the need to ensure they do no damage to others, indeed that they need to support their classmates when and how they can. Help children to consider use of language that will encourage collaboration and sharing, and language that isolates people. Find out what children think about helping their classmates as a way of helping themselves.

Use puppets to convey the idea that words can damage others; talk about feelings of confidence, caring and happiness, as well as anxiety, worry, fear and distrust.

Use whole-class talk to consider the children's perception of happiness, pleasure, interest and feeling worthy or important. Children should reflect upon the idea that everyone is equally important, no matter what. Stress that feelings change, and that feelings can helpfully be communicated.

Establish a conversation time where children have the opportunity to ask one another how they are feeling, what is worrying them, what they are looking forward to, what they like and dislike, how they might try to calm themselves if upset and so on. Model such talk with children so that they acquire the vocabulary to think about one another's feelings, and to express their own feelings. For example, take a topic such as 'Arguments', 'Self-worth' or 'I feel . . .' and go into detail about how and why to discuss perceptions and feelings with one another on a regular basis. You can link this with simple meditation sessions.

Arguments as disagreement

Model 'having an argument' with your TA. Try and include humour and asides to the class 'audience' so that they see what you are doing. Ask the children to talk with their group about how listening to an argument makes them feel, and what it feels like to argue with someone yourself. Model a way of resolving the argument by discussion, reasoning or negotiation, and ask children to analyse what happened. Ask children in groups to devise a role play in which they model an argument about a classroom topic such as who goes first in the queue, borrowing one another's property, winning and losing a game – show these to the class. Discuss the nature of arguments as a use of spoken language, what is useful and what is destructive, and what rules might apply.

Self-worth

Model 'showing off' and 'bragging' with your TA, along with self-deprecation and hopelessness. Ask the groups to analyse what happened. Provide children with the vocabulary to describe feeling rejected or fearing the future, and asking for support or thanking others for help. If you think the children can do so, ask them to devise and show a role play in which a child seems to 'know' everything; what if they have to admit they don't know? Discuss the plays.

'I feel . . .'

Ask children to talk to one another in their group, taking turns and starting with the words 'I feel . . .'. They can offer one word, a reason or a sentence. Listeners should show attentiveness to the feeling described. Children can start with four or five basic states of mind (e.g. angry, sad, happy, scared, fine) and try to think of examples of these feelings.

These states of mind can be elaborated or refined: angry (cross, upset), sad (unhappy, miserable), happy (excited, delighted), scared (frightened, worried), fine (confident, pleasant, uninterested). You can ask children to talk about whether they want to say how they feel, or not, and why.

In the 2015 Pixar Animation film *Inside Out* the key emotions are identified and personified as Joy, Sadness, Fear, Disgust and Anger. Children can usefully discuss these labels, and the characters, to decide if they would choose different labels or other emotion 'characters', and why. It is also helpful to talk about the graphic portrayal of characters, e.g. Sadness is coloured blue, slightly overweight, wears glasses and unattractive clothes, and has poor posture. Are all people with these characteristics 'sad'?

In this film, director Pete Docter conveys the idea that emotions are meant to connect people together, and that relationships are the most important things in life. There is much for children to talk about here. The link between individual resilience and independence, and true collaboration and support between classmates, is very important but rarely articulated.

Talk Box and geography

One of the aims of the geography curriculum is to enable children to begin to interpret sources of geographical information such as maps, globes and aerial photographs, amongst others. Through developing the use of simple geographical vocabulary, children can begin to discuss physical and human features, and understand and explain what simple maps and plans show. They can also begin to explore the use of symbols and keys.

Geography activity: A bird's eye view

This activity introduces the idea of a relationship between a simple map and an aerial view of a small and familiar area.

In the Talk Box	Small toy models of buildings – for example, Lilliput Lane houses or similar; Lego houses made by the children; city buildings constructed from Multilink
	A photograph of an aerial view of the school or a small section of the local area

Begin by talking to the children about what shape a 3D model of a house would make as a 'footprint' on the ground. You can draw round the model buildings on a piece of paper to explore this.

Now create a context in which you need to use a plan to explain to someone where a building is. Use examples from the photograph to discuss together how you might show some of the buildings on a plan. Encourage the children to think about how to represent a building, how to place it relative to other buildings and how to depict other contextual things such as roads, car parks, rivers, parkland or green space, trees, railway line, canal and so on.

Ask children to discuss plans by providing a copy of your aerial photograph that every group can see, and a set of Talking Points.

Talking Points: A bird's eye view

The roofs of the buildings look different because you can see more of them than when you look up from the ground.

A bird would see this if they were flying over.

> The trees and green spaces cover most of the picture.
>
> Buildings are usually very close together.
>
> Some things in the photograph are going to be there for a long time, but others are not.
>
> Another photograph taken at a different time would look different.
>
> You can see why things are where they are.
>
> It doesn't look like a picture of the school because . . .

Share points that children have made to help them to understand the idea of a plan.

Geographical talk

Provide each group with a copy of an aerial photograph. Now ask the children to talk together to agree a way of making a plan that shows the main features in the photograph, deciding what it is important to include.

Alternatively, ask the children to make a model of the photograph's features, using construction materials such as plasticine, Lego, air-drying clay or papier maché. Arrange the solid shapes on a board and draw in roads and other features. Discuss the difficulties of making a plan, and the point and purposes of plans.

Extension

Introduce the idea of a geographical key. Ask the children to think about how you could show features that are the same, for example trees, by making a symbol for use on the plan. They can then make a plan or an aerial photograph of an imaginary street, village or school, with a simple key to explain to others what their particular symbols mean. Talk about what makes a clear symbol.

Talk Box and art
: The art curriculum aims to encourage children to produce creative work, and to use the language of art, craft and design.

Art activity: Abstract
: This activity asks children to look together at a range of pictures, then discuss how they could use colour and materials to produce a shared collage.

In the Talk Box	Photographs of a range of abstract pictures, maybe using a range of media
	A range of materials such as a variety of fabric, string, wool, paper of a variety of textures and colours, card, glue, scissors, felt tips

Begin by discussing the examples of abstract art. Ask groups to consider what shapes the artist has used, and to what purpose. What is the background like? What materials might have been used? How is colour influencing the appearance of the image?

Now ask each group to choose one of the example pictures as a starting point. Explain that they need to talk together to agree on a plan for how this picture could be extended into a bigger shared picture that they will make together; perhaps they might place the picture in the centre of a larger piece of paper. They must then agree how to work together to build a bigger picture around it. They also need to agree which materials from the Talk Box to use in their creative work. Ask groups to discuss ideas and share this as a class before any practical work begins. In particular, ask groups to consider the importance of collaboration and what this might mean: does it mean division of labour with one person choosing materials, cutting, glueing and organising, with other people fetching and carrying?

After the groups have completed their shared picture, ask the children to say what they like about the other groups' finished pieces. Organise a plenary session in which children have the opportunity to consider their own achievements, and their group work. What was it like to work together on the same picture? Is there anything that was hard to agree on? What might they do differently next time to make it easier to work together well? Ask groups for examples of effective talk.

Talk Box and music

Music is a sort of language: familiarity and experience make it easier to understand. Find out what music children in your class listen to, and familiarise yourself with some of it. (*Author's note: dubstep still defeats me.*) It is counter-productive to try to like all the music children suggest; there is a need for a kind of privacy between generations in music, where we as adults are meant to be excluded from a child's musical world. But with the variety and interest of music, children can be inspired and enabled to access the back catalogue of various genres. You can never have too much music. As with computers, the range of experience children bring to class is very wide; you can use your musical experts to help others find music. Children may not often have the chance to talk about music, but providing such opportunities in your classroom may help to establish them as open-minded listeners and provide them with the wholesome mental resources that music offers.

When asking children to listen to music, the child with the shortest attention span should be considered as the one to cater for (within reason!). There is no point playing an entire classical piece as even those interested in the first minute or so will have drifted off entirely after the third movement. Talk to children about listening, how to listen and why the music is important. Provide them with 'advance organisers' such as a key musical phrase they can listen out for, or a change of tempo or volume to note. It will probably be best just to play music for one or two minutes, to ensure that they will want to hear more rather than wanting it to stop! Choose music that enhances your topic work – world music, music of a particular instrument or time, a child's suggestion, music about a particular creature, weather or colour – and build up a sequence of related music over time.

Music activity: Swan music

Teach children the vocabulary they will need in order to articulate their ideas about a particular type of music; for example, 'volume', 'tune', 'instruments', 'high/low pitch', 'story', 'rhythm' – and so on, depending on what music you choose. The children will also need working vocabulary to describe their response to the music they hear, using words such as 'enjoyed', 'interested', 'magical', 'mysterious', 'clear', 'simple', 'liked', 'preferred', 'imagined' (and their opposites). Talk about avoiding generalisations such as 'nice' and 'boring', and encourage children to use a thesaurus or word bank. Ask children what vocabulary any of them already know to describe music.

In the Talk Box	Swan music lasting 2–5 minutes (Sibelius, Gibbons, Saint-Saens, Tchaikovsky)
	Pictures of swans
	Swan toys/model animals
	Film of swans on water and in flight

Show the swans and describe the talk task, then play the music. Stop the music and ask the children to talk together to decide in their group:

- one thing they liked about the music;
- one thing they didn't like.

Make sure that every child has been asked for their opinion by others in the group. You can do this by having the children pass round a card (or toy swan) so that each child in turn speaks as they receive it. The groups then need to come to a decision or group agreement to share with the class. Ask groups to explain their thinking.

Give out swan toys or pictures, or show a video clip of swans. Now ask the children to decide by talking:

- three things they know about swans;
- three questions they would like to ask about swans.

Ask the class to share the knowledge they have discussed. Also, ask for and record the questions. Find out if any class members can answer any of the questions immediately; ask children to find out what they can about swans to answer other questions. Make a class blog, book or web page with the music as part of this.

Organise a plenary discussion in which children nominate others in their group as good listeners, those who gave interesting ideas, encouraged everyone to join in or those who asked thoughtful questions. Stress the importance of the talk as a way of making sure everyone got to know the music. Find out if the children would like to hear more of the piece, or have related suggestions that they'd like their classmates to share.

Chapter 9 # A variety of Talk Boxes

Stimulating educational discussion in a wide range of contexts. Teaching talk skills directly and providing opportunities for practice so that children become fluent in the use of talk for learning with a group.

In this chapter, we suggest use of a variety of boxes and resources that will provide a focus for discussion around your curricular activities. These can be adapted and extended, and no doubt you will have your own ideas about boxes and resources for talk.

Mini boxes – small plastic boxes (7 × 4 × 6 cm) with clip tops

Give each child, or each group, a mini box and ask them to use it to bring into school something they would like to talk about. Provide guidance on what is, and what is not, acceptable (e.g. no ladybirds or living things!). A good start is to bring in a mini box yourself. The boxes may have themes such as 'Feelings' for which children bring a written word or picture; 'Summer' for which they bring something they collected during the school holiday; 'Outdoors' for which they collect a stone, twig, leaf or similar; 'Books' for which they bring a book title or 'Antiques' for which they bring something old. Other themes could include treasure, a toy, the garden, the park, pets and other animals, hobbies, etc.

Each box is an opportunity to teach and learn talk skills such as questioning, describing and explaining. By helping to provide box contents, children are motivated to practice talking with others.

Take home boxes

1. Use a shoe box and a toy animal, preferably one that has character rather than anything too 'cute' or anything linked to a movie. Include a notebook and pencil in the box. Start by sharing the character with the class, asking for a name and telling the children that they will have a chance to take the box home and write or draw a diary entry. Ensure that the children respect the character and feel drawn to taking it home. Choose a child to take the box home on a Friday for the weekend, bringing it back no later than Tuesday. Ask them to write a sentence, or draw a picture, to show how the character shared a family meal, outing, game, film or programme. Family members can be invited to help. Continue until all children have taken the character home, sharing stories about what happened.

2. Provide something relevant to your topic in a small box, envelope or disposable cup (whatever is suitable). Ask children to take home the item with a suggested activity. Allow time for children to share the item at home. Ask children to share with their group what happened, and ask groups to explain their stories to the class.

Ask children for further take-home suggestions.

Examples of things to take home and talk about include: sunflower seeds; a bulb or corm; a folded origami snapper, box or bird; a pencil; a slip of paper with a web link to a song or story; a 2p or foreign coin; pictures cut from a comic or magazine; stickers; an animal toy or picture; three different leaves; a paper clip and an elastic band (make a machine); a postcard.

DIY box

Provide (or ask children to provide) a shoe box, cereal box or egg box – any sort of reasonably robust, medium-sized cardboard box packaging. To serve as an example, you might want to cover your box in wrapping paper or silver paper, with stickers or a label. The box needs to have a lid or hinged flap so that its contents are secure. The idea of the DIY box activity is to ask children to make their own box into something different from how it started out. What it turns into can depend on your topic, or it can be individual or imaginative. For example, children could make a car; a den; a house for a pet, alien or fairy; a cage; a seed tray; a treasure box; a word box (with words the child has collected inside); a box to hold books, stationery, paint and brushes; a CD or DVD; an emergency kit (torch, plasters, water bottle, pencil, notebook, etc.); a first aid kit; a box for a car, train or plane journey; a present for a child in hospital.

Ask children to talk together to plan and decide whether to share ideas or work separately. Children can take the DIY boxes home to work on, or bring in materials they need, or provide you with a list of things that they think will help them. The talk is about the construction, the idea behind the box and sharing the finished article, rather than acquiring possessions to put in the box.

Colour box

Use a shoe box or plastic box. Collect things that are all one colour. Include one or more Talking Points in the box for children to discuss.

Talking Points: One colour

We can sort these things into groups.

We can choose three things and make up a story.

We can say what materials the things are made of and why.

We can say why the things are this colour.

We can make a collage using only this colour.

We can spell the colour's name and words that are similar.

We can talk together to write a colour poem or make a colour picture.

Shape box

Collect a set of 2D and 3D shapes into a box. You might begin with separate sets and boxes depending on your class.

Provide one or more Talking Points in the box.

Talking Points: Shape box

We can name these shapes.

We can make up sentences using the words:

'edge', 'face', 'vertex', 'height', 'depth', 'volume'.

We can make a pattern by drawing round the shapes.

We can make a symmetrical pattern by drawing round the shapes.

We can make a tessellating pattern by drawing round the shapes.

We can say where these shapes are found in parts of the school buildings.

Once children have discussed their ideas about the shapes, have handled the shapes and listened to their classmates, they will be more ready to learn about them, and you will have more idea what it is that they need to learn.

Touch box

Provide a box for each group containing materials that have a range of textured surfaces, such as paper towel, greaseproof or baking paper, sandpaper, silver paper, cotton wool, bandage, fur fabric, wool, stone, plastic, metal, wood, cork. If feeling really adventurous you could include something wet, sticky, gritty or squishy/flexible.

Ask children to talk together to make up some questions about how the materials feel. Help groups to ask the whole class their questions and discuss answers; highlight accurate vocabulary use.

Use some Talking Points such as the following to extend discussion:

Talking Points: Materials

Wet materials are always cold.

You can feel things best with the palms of your hands.

Knowing how things feel helps us to stay safe.

Rough surfaces are always a nuisance.

Collection box

It's always interesting to make a collection. Children may have their own collections of particular toys, cards, erasers, DVDs, books and so on. Parents may have collections that they are willing to lend you or come in to talk about. Bring in your own collection; describe it, say what the things mean to you and show how it is of value. I once saw a teacher do this with six egg cups, and it was truly fascinating and really fired the children's imagination.

Collections can be complete or ongoing, fragile or robust, expensive or quite affordable. A class can start a collection at the beginning of a school year. There will always be lots to talk about with a collection. Suitable things for a class to collect are, for example, postcards (these are cheap and children can bring one in when they go anywhere), stamps, food packaging labels, particularly shaped objects, mugs, photos, books, comics, spoons, exciting pictures, 'antiques', pencil sharpeners or erasers – whatever suits your class and your topic.

In the Talk Box

Collections

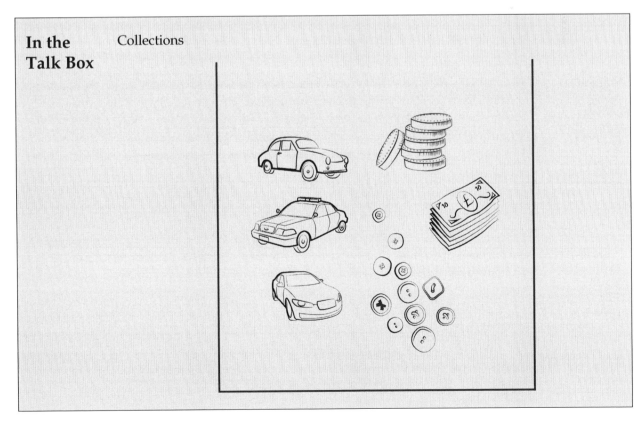

The collection will have to be carefully curated and organised. This process can generate some useful discussion about ownership, responsibility, sharing, cataloguing, access and so on.

Individual children, or groups, can make a collection. They can use appropriate vocabulary to describe, organise and share their collection, and talk about their own perception of, and interest in, the collection.

Provide a shoe box and ask children to start a collection that reflects their own interests, e.g. shells, erasers, CDs, beads, foreign coins and notes, badges, buttons, stickers, toy cars – children will have their own ideas about such things. Ask children to research information and share this information by describing and explaining. They should be able to talk about their collection, use their resource for creative writing and ask relevant questions about another collection. This can be an ongoing activity in a classroom.

Food and drink box

(Note: ensure that you are fully aware of children's food allergies and dietary restrictions.)

Link your topic to appropriate food and drink. Bring in a box of taster samples of food or drink and ask children to describe taste and smell using accurate vocabulary, e.g. 'salty', 'bitter', 'sweet', 'acidic', 'spicy', 'scented' and so on. Link the types of food under focus with curriculum topics that you are studying, such as specific countries and cultures. Link also with fruits and seeds, or consider varieties of staple food such as bread.

Packaging for food

Set up group discussions to find out what children think about logos and advertising. Ask groups to look at the energy, salt or sugar contained in foods. Look at packaging and discuss how individuals might reduce the use of packaging, and why this is necessary.

Lunch box

Talk about healthy eating, food ingredients and energy values. Provide packets so that children can look up, talk about and compare the ingredients of particular foods, such as lemonade, crisps, biscuits or burgers.

Boxes of games

Use board games, quizzes and card games, even traditional games such as dominoes or ludo. Discuss rules with the children, and ask them to consider how games differ when played collaboratively (i.e. in teams) or individually and competitively. Organise a 'beat the game' session by having all players share and talk about what is happening. Find out who prefers team collaboration compared to individual play, and in what contexts. Winning and losing at board games can be a very emotional experience, as evidenced by the behaviour of some adults! Most of us need help to learn to be a graceful winner or unresentful loser in a game, and discussing the game itself, its rules and aims, and feelings of winning and losing, can help children to keep taking part in playing games. Box games can be stimulating, interesting and educational in a range of ways, and at best can really help children to socialise and have fun with others.

Other boxes

The range of box types is quite astonishing, and all can be roped in to help us support curriculum learning, and help children learn to talk with one another. You can devise creative and useful activities with pencil boxes (history, materials), egg boxes (forces, animal welfare), presents (festivals, gifts, packaging), boxes at the theatre (history, music), box files, a recipe box, veg box, TV Smart Box, drop box, cash box, telephone box, jury box, horsebox, tick box . . .

Chapter 10   Classic Talk Box activities

A selection of updated and revised ideas and activities for integrating talk into class work, taken from the Talk Box *2004 edition.*

Provide or display a copy of p. 92 **'Talk Box cue cards'** or print on cards.

Talk Box cue cards

These cards help children to get used to the structures of Exploratory Talk when working in a group. Laminate and cut separate cards. Start with the cards 'My turn to talk' and two or three 'My turn to listen' cards. Ask children to choose who starts with the talk card, and set up your talk activity. Now the children take it in turns to take a card, noting and doing as it says, before passing the cards on to their neighbour when they are ready, or when asked. Allow time for the discussion to flow. In your closing plenary, check if the children found the cards to be a helpful reminder. Maybe coloured cards, instead of cards with words, would suit them better?

Go on to using the 'What do you think?' / 'Why do you think that?' cards. Help children to see that by asking a direct question, they can help their classmates to provide information, explain or elaborate, and the 'Why?' question helps everyone to think about using reasons in discussion. Children can begin to make decisions about whether they agree with reasons and think they are based on evidence, or decide if they feel some reasons are 'better' than others.

Progress to using the 'I agree' / 'I disagree' cards once the groups are able to sustain a conversation. Teach children that they can disagree with ideas rather than disagreeing with people, and that reasons are essential in an educationally effective discussion. Teach the cordial and encouraging use of the words 'why' and 'because' in this setting. 'I can explain' and 'I can sum up' require the child to offer an oral response, but this is in a supportive group setting, and based on collaborative talk. Turn taking with these cards ensures that all voices are heard, and that confidence is built.

The children will soon grow out of the cards as they internalise these talk tools, and build them into their own vocabularies and strategies for talking to others. It is always useful to ask for positive feedback for group mates after a discussion. For example, asking questions such as 'Who asked you a good question?', 'Who helped you to feel included?', 'Who listened to you, and how could you tell?' and 'Who explained clearly?' all provide chances for children to support one another's talk competence.

Talk Box sharing

This activity encourages children to ask one another direct questions, to find out a little more about each other and to identify what they have in common with one another. Print or display the resource **'We all like'** found on p. 93.

In groups of three, ask children to write their name next to one of the smiley faces. Ask two of the children to find out what they both like. You can give the class a theme, such as films, books, food, animals, hobbies, games, days out, holidays – or the topic can be open. Once the two children have found out their shared likes, they note them in 'their' arrow. The third child listens and helps by asking questions or giving prompts. Then the first child becomes the listener, and children two and three discuss what they share. Finally, children three and one talk together. Once this has happened, the children can fill in the central section by drawing or writing what they have in common.

Children could go on to swap groups and try again with others. Ask them to suggest a topic to talk about. In your plenary, find out if children were surprised to find that they liked the same things. Ask groups to give feedback on how difficult or easy it was to talk together, and to nominate group mates who are 'good listeners', 'good to talk to', 'friendly and helpful', and so on. You could use this activity to help you to establish effective talk groups. Children can take a copy of the resource home to share with family: they could try it with four in the group.

A story to talk about: *Ribby Rabbit Goes First*

Provide or display a copy of p. 91 **'Rabbit finger puppets'** or print on cards.

In the Talk Box	Toy rabbits, pictures of rabbits Rabbit finger puppets

Whole-class work 1

Ask children what they know about rabbits – real or imaginary. Select a rabbit from the box and give it one of the rabbit characters' names from the story. You will need nine children to hold up the puppet rabbits while the story is being read. Alternatively, give one rabbit to each group or one finger puppet to each child.

Group work

Read the story *Ribby Rabbit Goes First* and ask the children to hold up the character rabbit when it appears in the story. Ask the children to say what they thought of how Ribby and Kipling behaved.

Groups can now talk together to:

a) make up another scene in the story, or a different ending;
b) act out the story as a play;
c) draw Ribby and write ten describing words around the picture.

Whole-class work 2

Ask the class to share their work, with children concentrating on listening, asking questions and providing positive feedback for one another.

Ribby Rabbit Goes First

Ribby always wanted to be first in the queue. All the rabbits in Miss Thistle's class were fed up of him. Whenever they had to stand in a line, Ribby would rush to the front, shoving everyone else out of the way.

'Me first! Me first!' shouted Ribby.

There were six rabbits in Miss Thistle's class: Ribby and his twin sister Blackberry; the triplets Kipling, Lemony and Muzzle; and Bramble Bunny.

On Monday, Miss Thistle asked the class to line up for break.

'Me first!' shouted Ribby, hopping up so rapidly that he knocked over a basket of pencils. They scattered on the floor and all their points broke. Everyone had to pick them up while Ribby stood crossly at the door.

On Tuesday, Miss Thistle asked the class to line up to have their photos taken. 'Me first!' shouted Ribby, shoving his chair back so hard that it crashed to the ground. Muzzle picked it up for him. Ribby was so determined to be first that he didn't have time to do it himself.

On Wednesday, Miss Thistle asked the class to line up for assembly.

'Me first!' shouted Ribby, leaping to the door in such a rush that he banged into Lemony and she started to cry. Then Kipling lost his temper. He jumped up and shoved Ribby so hard that he fell over. Bramble Bunny thought this wasn't fair and with a great push he knocked Kipling down, so Muzzle dashed across and crashed into Bramble – and suddenly all six rabbits were tumbling around the classroom. It took Miss Thistle and the class quite a while to sort it all out.

'Right,' said Miss Thistle. 'We are going to have to do something differently.'

On Thursday, Miss Thistle said, 'Ribby, please stay in your place. Everyone else line up for lunch.' The rabbits got themselves into a line. Ribby frowned so hard that his ears stood straight up. 'Now Ribby, please join the end of the line,' said Miss Thistle. Ribby stamped across the room (and don't forget that a rabbit's feet are rather large). 'It's not fair!' he said to Kipling, who was just in front of him. 'Hey. Don't worry so much,' said Kipling. 'What does it matter?'

Ribby couldn't explain why it mattered. But it did. They all went outside for lunch, which was a dandelion sandwich and chocolate cake. Ribby was last in line. When it was finally his turn, Fluff said, 'Are you the last? You might as well have all of this then!' and she gave Ribby a really big slice of cake. He liked that. But after lunch, Miss Thistle said, 'Please come here and sit down, Ribby,' and he had to wait on the grass until all the others had lined up.

'Please join the back of the line, Ribby.'

Ribby didn't like everyone going in before him. He frowned and grumbled to himself. But as he went through the door, Head Rabbit Mr Marjoram came along. Ribby held the door for him. 'Well, thank you Ribby,' said Mr Marjoram. 'Will you take a message for me? Tell Miss Thistle and the class that Swizzle the storyteller will be arriving in half an hour.' This was great news. When Ribby told Miss Thistle and the others, they were all very excited and pleased with him. It was almost as if he had been the one that had organised the treat.

The bell rang.

'Please line up for the storyteller!' said Miss Thistle.

Of course Ribby immediately jumped up.

'Me . . . . . .!!!' he began. But he stopped in mid jump. Something funny had happened. All the other rabbits had lined up, but they'd left a big space at the front of the line. They were keeping the place at the front especially for him. Why? Ribby wasn't so sure he liked this.

'Why are they all trying to make me go first?' he thought. 'It must be because no-one else wants to be first. Perhaps it isn't a good thing to go at the front!' He ignored the space and went to the end of the line.

'Ribby, you are funny,' said Kipling. Ribby, who was the last to sit down on the grass, liked having a big space to himself. They all enjoyed sitting outside and listening to the storyteller.

On Friday, Miss Thistle was looking forward to a quiet day with everyone having a nice time in class. It was sunny outside and the bees were buzzing about. Everyone seemed happy and relaxed.

At half past ten she said, 'Please will everyone line up for break?'

Then it happened. 'ME LAST!!' shouted Ribby, dashing to the back of the classroom and tipping over two tables on the way. 'ME LAST!'

Poem: *Fairy Story* **by Stevie Smith**

In the Talk Box	A copy or display version of the poem
	A copy of the Talking Points for each group
	Coloured pencils or felt tips
	A selection of 'little creatures' (as in the poem: pictures or models of, e.g., frog, goblin, alien, mouse, worm, pixie, hobbit, hedgehog, beetle)
	Tape/CD with suitable music, e.g. theme from *The Lord of the Rings*, an Enya song, a short piece of flute music, etc.

A poem to talk about: *Fairy Story* **by Stevie Smith**

Whole class

Display and read the poem aloud.

Fairy Story

I went into the wood one day
And there I walked and lost my way

When it was so dark I could not see
A little creature came to me

He said if I would sing a song
The time would not be very long

But first I must let him hold my hand tight
Or else the wood would give me a fright

I sang a song, he let me go
But now I am home again there is nobody I know.

Whole-class work

Ask the children to talk and think together in their group:

a) look at or listen to the Talking Points and decide whether they agree, disagree or are unsure about the statements, giving reasons and finding out what everyone in their group thinks. Share their ideas with the class;

b) draw, make a collage picture or use a graphics program; use word labels (annotate) to show how they imagine the setting, the creature and the writer;

c) listen to the music and think of some simple song words;

d) decide what has happened at the end of the poem. Discuss ideas with the whole class;

e) talk about walking alone/getting lost/relying on strangers to help;

f) use the rhymes that Stevie Smith uses: day, way; see, me; song, long; tight, fright; go, know.
Try to devise a poem of their own using these rhymes.
This can be a 'fairy story' or an adventure, a dream, a description, a list of ideas about woodland or a magic poem about one of the little creatures.

Talking Points: *Fairy Story*

- We know what has happened! We can share ideas. This is our idea about what happened to make everyone at home seem like a stranger . . .
- We know what happens next! This is our idea . . .
- We know what the little creature looks like! We can draw it and write some describing words.
- We know what song to sing! We can suggest ideas and record them.
- We can share stories about when we were scared.
- We can think of scary things! We can draw four things that might be frightening in the woods at night.
- We can think of magic creatures! We can draw a magic _____ to help us in the woods. We can say what it does.

A PSHE story to talk about: *Climbing Frame Tag*

In the Talk Box	Playground pictures/model of a climbing frame
	5 pictures, models or dolls to represent the children
	Toy dog
	Green ball
	8 story pictures and *Climbing Frame Tag* story to read, or perhaps recorded

Resources:

Provide one a copy of p. 95 per group: '*Climbing Frame Tag:* **How do the children feel?'**

Provide or display a copy of p. 96 '**Story scenes**' and p. 97 '**Story characters**' or print on cards.

Whole-class work 1

Use Talk Box resources to talk with children about trips to the park. Ask them to share ideas about if and why they enjoy going, and who with.

Ask children to suggest Ground Rules for use when asking questions or talking together to come to a group agreement.

Ask the children to listen carefully to the story *Climbing Frame Tag*. Before reading, provide this introduction to the story, showing pictures **'Story scenes'** and **'Story characters'**.

Introduction

There are five children in this story: Arsha, Erin, Declan, Vijay and Sally.

While you are listening to the story, try to think of how the children might be **feeling** while different things happen. Do you think that they are happy, sad, upset, excited, friendly, cross or lonely?

Group work

a) Ask groups to discuss the story and then to complete or suggest ideas using `How do the children feel?'. They can draw, write or explain their group response.

b) Allocate a story picture and a character to each group. Ask children to talk together to decide what their character did in the story, why they think they did that and what else they could have done instead. Remind children to share all their ideas and to provide each other with reasons.

Whole-class work 2

Ask groups to share their thinking. Invite the groups to explain what they decided about the choices the characters made.

What did the children in the story do and what could they have chosen to do instead? What would you do? Can you say why?

Ask groups to report how well they felt they worked together. Who asked a question? Did anyone have to change their mind about what they first thought? Can they think of examples of how they used the Ground Rules in their discussion?

Extension 1: Story ending

Resources: Large paper and felt tip pens/drawing program.

Ask the groups to talk together and draw a picture which shows:

a) their idea for an ending to the story – What happens when Erin gets home? Where does the ball end up? What is the end of the story from Shep's point of view?

b) their ideas for another episode of the story – What happens if Vijay is given a new ball to take to the park?

Ask groups to make up a one-minute play or freeze-frame that will show their story ending.

Extension 2: Follow-up for group reasoning

Ask the children to think together to choose a character and episode from the story. Record how the character is feeling. Think what could happen to make the character's feelings change: What could another character do? Why? Record their new version of the story.

Extension 3: Follow-up for individual reasoning

Ask the children to work individually.

Ask the children to think about what they liked and disliked about the story and to record this, with their reasons. For example, they could colour characters they liked green and those they disliked red, then record a reason. Ask the children to explain their thoughts to a partner, group or adult. What are good reasons? What reasons do people share?

Climbing Frame Tag

Arsha, Declan and Erin were at the park. They were playing with Erin's green ball. They made up a really good game around the climbing frame, throwing the ball to each other and rolling it down the slide. Vijay came along, and watched for a minute.

'Come and join in,' said Erin. She threw him the ball.

Vijay caught the ball, but instead of throwing it back he held on to it. Then, without a word, he kicked it away and ran off, booting it ahead of him. They called but he kept on running till he reached the far end of the park. Their game was over and the park didn't seem like a good place to be.

'Well,' said Declan. 'He took the ball, he took the game.'

Vijay played with the ball by himself for a while. It didn't seem a very interesting thing to do on his own. There was no-one to kick it to, or throw it back to him. Sally arrived in the park and watched him for a minute.

'Come and join in,' said Vijay.

Back at the climbing frame, the others were deciding what to do.

'But we can still play,' said Arsha. 'We can start again and make up a new game.' They began to play a complicated sort of tag around the climbing frame, making up new rules and making sure everyone got caught.

'Ok, I'll play,' said Sally to Vijay. He kicked the green ball towards her. Sally threw it up in the air, caught it, and set off running away as fast as she could.

'Hey!' shouted Vijay. He ran after Sally but she was much faster than he was; he just had to stop and watch her go. He knew he'd never catch her. Now he was on his own again, with no-one to play with and nothing to do. Kicking a stone, he made his way slowly back to where the others were playing climbing frame tag.

'Hey! Where's my ball?' called Erin.

'Sally took it off me,' said Vijay.

'Oh, just come and play,' said Declan. 'We can get it back later.'

'I don't know the rules,' said Vijay.

'You learn them by playing. We just change them if we like,' said Asha. 'All you have to do is go up the slide, not down, and I'm it, so you'd better run . . .' Vijay made a dash for the slide and in a moment they were all running and climbing and sliding. It was a good game.

It was Erin who first saw Sally running towards them over the grass, flying along as if she was being chased. The game stopped again while they watched. It looked as if she was coming to join in but taking no notice of anyone, Sally ran right under the slide and hid herself there, making puffing noises to get her breath back.

'OK Sally! Where's the ball?' said Vijay. Sally shook her head.

'What are you doing under there?' said Erin. Sally crept out from her hiding place looking anxiously the way she had come.

'There was a dog, a horrible, fierce dog,' she said. 'I was rolling the ball along and a big brown dog came and it just grabbed it and took it away. It growled at me and I thought it was going to bite – it didn't have an owner, there was no-one I could ask for help –'

Declan climbed to the top of the climbing frame and looked around. He shook his head. No sign of any dog.

'It's gone now, Sally,' said Arsha. 'You'd better stay with us for a while. It probably won't bother us if we're all together.'

It took a while, but eventually Sally calmed down a bit.

'Sorry about your ball,' she said to Vijay. He looked a bit ashamed.

'It wasn't mine,' he said. 'I don't know whose it is.' The others looked at Erin but funnily enough she didn't seem too worried.

'I brought it to play with,' she said. 'But it isn't mine either. It belongs to our dog, Shep. He loves it.' The children thought maybe they should have looked after the dog's favourite toy a bit better.

'You know what?' said Sally. 'I bet that brown dog was one of Shep's friends, and Shep sent him to bring the ball back for him!'

They played the game of climbing frame tag together till it was time to go home.

Chapter 11   Assessment of children's talk for learning

Straightforward ways for you and the children to reflect on and evaluate talk.

Assessment

Children's talk with you during whole-class sessions or during group activities can be used to assess not only their spoken language skills but also their learning in curriculum subjects. Talk Box activities provide useful opportunities for formative assessment. Formative assessment can take place while children are in discussion with yourself or each other, as you listen to individuals or groups and collect information about their understanding and skills. Such everyday assessment can help you to adapt what you have planned to meet the needs you have identified. Intervention to challenge misconceptions and provide further information can then be accurately focused.

You may want to identify and work on specific aspects of children's talking and thinking. **'Questions for teacher assessment during group work'** suggests some features of talk that you can observe and note. Your aims for the assessment will affect how these questions are used. For example, you may wish to concentrate on a child or children who have difficulty in speaking and listening, or may wish to conduct a whole-class audit of talk. The list can be used to compile a tally as group work proceeds, as an everyday checklist to have in mind, or for yourself or your TA to audit a particular child or children.

Teacher assessment of talk in class

Questions for teacher assessment during group work

1. Does the child initiate and carry on conversations?
2. Does the child listen carefully?
3. Can the child's talk be easily understood?
4. Can the child describe experiences?
5. Can the child give instructions?
6. Does the child follow verbal instructions?
7. Does the child modify talk for different audiences?
8. Does the child ask questions?
9. Does the child give reasons?
10. Does the child ask others for their views?
11. Does the child reply to challenging questions with reasons?
12. Can the child take joint responsibility for decisions?
13. Can the child 'think aloud'?
14. Can the child generate and consider an alternative point of view?

Each of these questions could be used to consider the child's talk in more detail by taking each question and going in to much more depth. This can be useful if the assessment is to be used diagnostically to identify particular areas of strength or weakness.

As an example, '**More detailed questions for teacher assessment**' takes assessment question 2 ('Does the child listen carefully?') and sets out to collect some more specific information. You can do this with any of the assessment questions.

More detailed questions for teacher assessment: Listening

Does the child listen carefully to a familiar adult; to an unfamiliar adult; to friends; to unfamiliar children; when working in a group; in a whole-class situation; in a whole-school situation; not usually; almost always?

Can the child respond to what they hear?

Self-evaluation by children

Children can usefully reflect on their talk skills and share their ideas with the class. These suggestions for closing plenary questions can help children to reflect on the quality of their talk after discussion sessions.

Plenary questions after a Talk Box session

What did you talk about?

Did you ask a question?

What do you remember someone else saying?

How did the Talk Rules help you to talk about this activity?

How did sharing your ideas help you?

Did it all go wrong; if so, what can we do differently?

How did sharing your ideas help your group?

Did your group reach a decision? Did the rules help you to do this?

What were other possibilities? Why did your group reject these?

Can you provide an example of a good reason/question/challenge you heard today?

Who did you notice acting as a good listener? How can we tell?

Did you or any of your group change your mind about something? Can you say why?

Self-assessment using a Talk Diary

More formal self-assessment can be used to build up a comprehensive picture of the child's opportunities to talk with others in a range of contexts. A Talk Diary can focus children on the importance of their talk, providing a useful resource for analysis or reporting. The Talk Diary can be completed, for example, at the end of each Talk Box session, at the end of the day for a week of term, or intermittently to suit your purposes. Children can record what they have experienced with ticks and crosses; or they can evaluate their own experience using a number or colour system. They can use colour dot stickers or smiley faces. It's useful on occasion to talk with children as they complete a Talk Diary and note their comments.

Here is a suggested format for the Talk Diary:

ASSESSMENT OF CHILDREN'S TALK FOR LEARNING

Talk Diary

Name		Start Date	

Talk Box Lesson Numbers

	1	2	3	4	5
I talked to the whole class					
I talked in a group					
I asked a question					
I answered a question					
I gave a reason					
I said what I thought					
I listened carefully					
My group talked well					
I joined in					
I liked talking to my group					
I found it hard to talk					
I found it hard to listen					
We could not agree					
We decided together					

Appendix

Photocopiable worksheets

Are these useful Ground Rules for Talk? What do you think?

1
We will take turns to talk and to listen

2
We will have a leader and do as they say

3
Everyone will talk as loud as they can

4
We will ask each other questions

5
We will agree with our friends and disagree with everyone else

6
We are going to try to beat each other

7
We will respect each other's ideas

8
If we don't agree it doesn't matter

9
You don't have to join in if you don't want to

10
If you have a good idea, you can interrupt

11
We will try to share what we know

12
We will listen and think about each other's ideas

Worksheet 1 Are these useful Ground Rules for Talk?

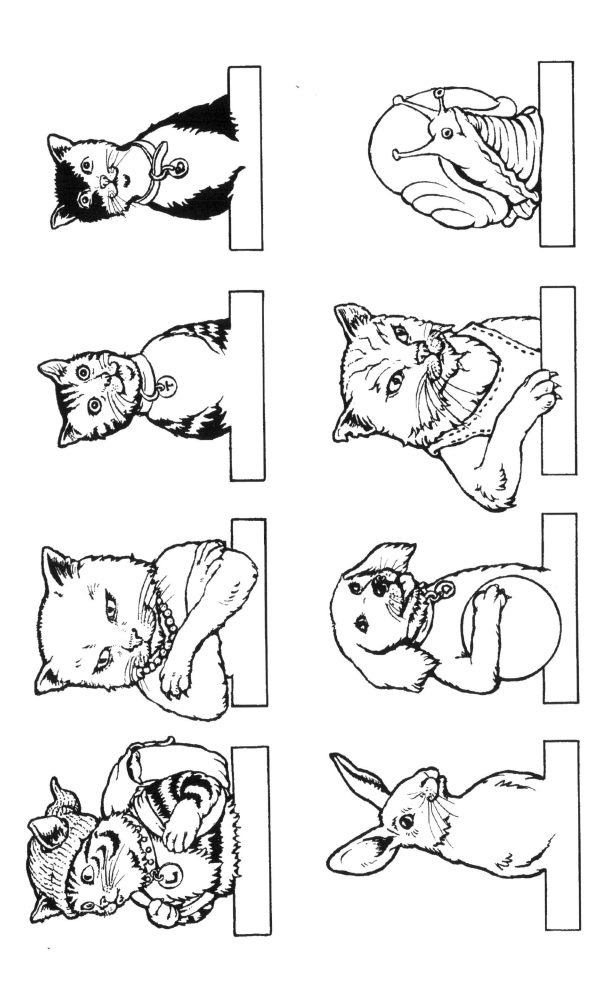

Worksheet 2   Liffey finger puppets

My turn to
talk

My turn to
listen

What do you
think?

Why do you
think that?

I agree with

....

because ....

I don't agree with

....

because ....

I can
explain

I can sum up
what we said

Worksheet 3   Talk Box cue cards

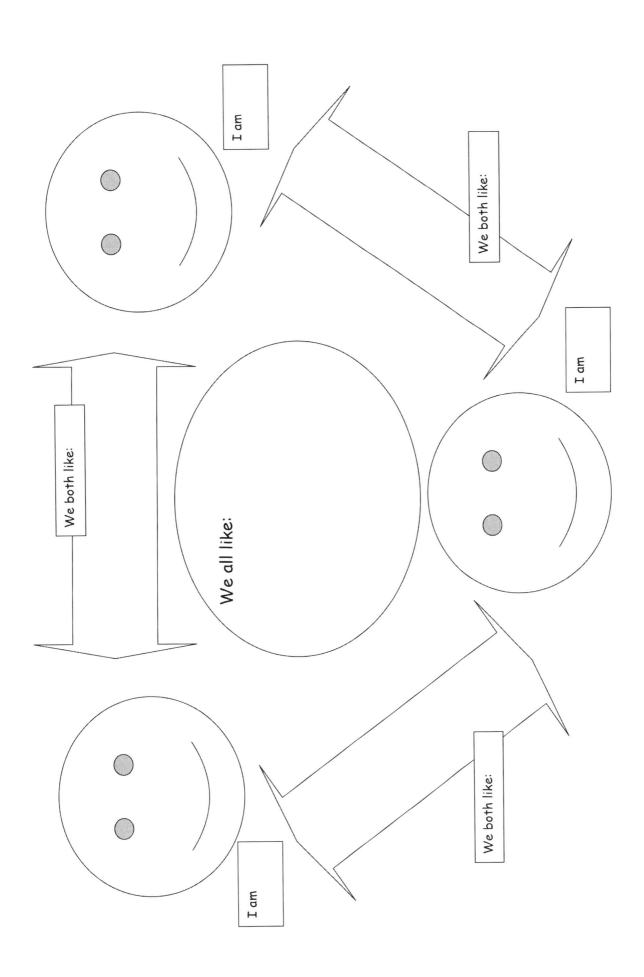

Worksheet 4   We all like

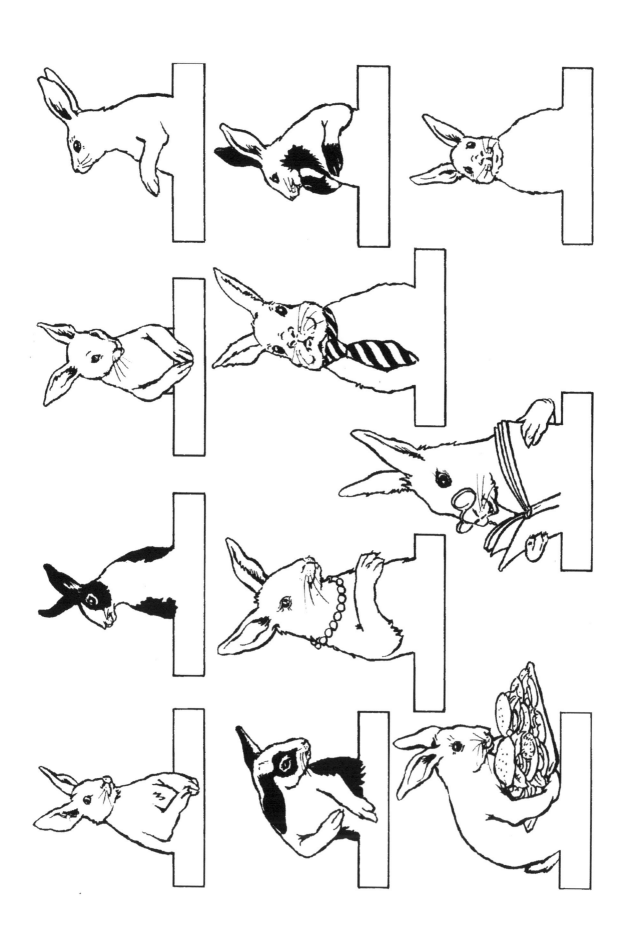

	Arsha	Erin	Declan	Vijay	Sally
1. Climbing frame game					
2. Vijay runs away					
3. Sally arrives in the park					
4. Climbing frame tag					
5. Sally runs away					
6. Vijay joins in					
7. Sally's story					
8. Shep's Friend					

Worksheet 6   *Climbing Frame Tag*: How do the children feel?

Worksheet 7 Story scenes

Sally

Vijay

Declan

Arsha

Erin

Worksheet 8   Story characters

Talk Box links and references

Home-School Links

We have mentioned ideas that children can carry home to talk about throughout the book. You can ensure that children are motivated to talk with others at home and that there are opportunities to come back and share what they have learned or discussed. Extending conversation about learning into the child's home can be tricky. But helping the child to see that school and home are not completely different worlds can promote a sense of belonging and help to put curriculum learning into context. Talking about a book, a science lesson, a friend or a problem with someone at home can make all the difference to a child's developing capacity to understand. Websites for parents offer some imaginative ways to help children talk about school which you might adapt and use. The question 'How did you get on at school today?' has become a cliché – but its prevalence indicates that parents really do want to talk with their child about their experiences at school.

1. Written prompts

Ask children to take home a prompt for discussion or enquiry at home. This could be one or more of the day's Talking Points, a poem, paragraph or mathematical idea to think aloud about, something to find out or something to share. Children's art work, drafts for stories, or plans for science investigations or D&T projects are valuable resources for discussion.

2. Oral prompts

Children can use their memories to carry questions and puzzles home. Use the motivation that your stimulating classroom activities create. Encourage children to think about a question, to say how they would describe or explain something, to memorise a phrase or an idea, to define a new word in their vocabulary, to plan a future activity, or to think about something they have heard or seen. This is what they can take home. Ask them to think of someone they are going to talk to. Try to enable children to give feedback from their home conversations, and to keep this conversation going over time.

Web links

Bradford Talking Schools

Bradford have pioneered excellent strategies for promoting oracy in all their schools. https://bso.bradford.gov.uk/Schools/Home.aspx

Cambridge Primary Review (CPR)

The CPR provides evidence to evaluate learning and teaching: for example, highlighting the value of dialogic teaching and the impact of direct teaching of talk skills. http://cprtrust.org.uk

The Communications Trust

The Communication Trust is a coalition of over fifty not-for-profit organisations. Working together, the CT supports everyone who works with children and young people in England to support their speech, language and communication. https://www.thecommunicationtrust.org.uk

Learning, Playing and Interacting

It may not always be clear how play and direct teaching work together – this useful document answers some difficult questions and stresses the value of talking with children.
www.keap.org.uk/documents/LearningPlayingInteracting.pdf

Oracy Assessment Toolkit

These materials provide a toolkit for assessing how well children of 11–12 years old can use spoken English for different purposes and in different contexts. They act as a model for the assessment of younger children.
www.educ.cam.ac.uk/research/projects/oracytoolkit

talkingpartners@primary

talkingpartners@primary (formerly known as Talking Partners) is a programme designed to improve the way children communicate across the curriculum, enabling them to be independent and skilful speakers and listeners.
www.educationworks.org.uk/what-we-do/speaking-and-listening/talking-partners.html

Talk Less Teaching

The idea here is that the teacher can spend less time talking to (rather disengaged) whole classes. Strategies for cutting down on too much teacher talk are tackled here with flair, encouraging children to express ideas and work collaboratively – but always acknowledging that the teacher is crucial.
http://osiriseducational.co.uk/staffroom/article/talk-less-teaching

Thinking Together

Spoken language enables us to do much more than share information – it enables us to **think together**. But as teachers, do we always use it to best advantage? And do we give enough attention to enabling children to use **language as a tool for learning and problem solving**?

On this website we explain how years of practical, **classroom-based research** in several countries and with learners of all ages has provided useful answers to these questions.

We also provide some **downloadable material** for researchers and teachers, with links to useful books, research projects and other websites.
https://thinkingtogether.educ.cam.ac.uk

Books

Brown, K. (2001) *The Scarecrow's Hat*. Atlanta, GA: Peachtree Publishers.
Carle, E. (2002 [1969]) *The Very Hungry Caterpillar*. London: Puffin.
Dawes, L. (2012) *Talking Points: Discussion Activities in the Primary Classroom*. London: Routledge.
Dawes, L. and Sams, C. (2004) *Talk Box*. London: David Fulton Press.
Goodwin, P (Ed) (2017) *The Articulate Classroom* (Classic Edition). Abingdon: Routledge.
Smith, S. (1987) 'Fairy Story', in M. Rogers (Ed.) *A Children's Book of Verse*. Newmarket, UK: Brimax Books.